The Global Business Game:

A Strategic Management and International Business Simulation, 2e

Player's Manual

Joseph Wolfe, Ph.D.

Experiential Adventures LLC
Professor Emeritus, University of Tulsa

THOMSON ™
SOUTH-WESTERN

Australia · Canada · Mexico · Singapore · Spain · United Kingdom · United States

Player's Manual for The Global Business Game, 2e
Joseph Wolfe

Editor-in-Chief:
Jack W. Calhoun

Team Leader:
Michael P. Roche

Executive Editor:
John Szilagyi

Media Technology Editor:
Vicky True

Sr. Marketing Manager:
Rob Bloom

Production Editor:
Daniel C. Plofchan

Media Developmental Editor:
Kristen Meere

Media Production Editor:
Karen L. Schaffer

Manufacturing Coordinators:
Rhonda Utley
Sandee Milewski

Compositor:
Bookcomp, Inc. / Nighthawk Design

Printer:
Victor Graphics
Baltimore, MD

Design Project Manager:
Christy Carr

Internal Designer:
Ramsdell Design/Craig Ramsdell,
Cincinnati

Cover Designer:
Christy Carr

Cover Photographer/Illustrator:
Christy Carr

Library of Congress Cataloging-in-
Publication Data
Wolfe, Joseph A. (Joseph Allen), 1935–
The global business game : a strategic
management and international business
simulation : player's manual / Joseph
Wolfe.—2nd ed.
p. cm.
Designed as a companion vol. to Strate-
gic management by Michael A. Hitt . . .
but may be used as a stand-alone game.
Includes index.
ISBN 0-324-16183-2
1. Management—Study and teaching—
Simulation methods. I. Title.
HD30.4 .W65 2002
658.4′0352—dc21

2002066863

Text ISBN: 0-324-16185-9
Package ISBN: 0-324-16183-2

To my wife, Nancy,
who has made possible so many wonderful experiences

Contents

List of Exhibits and Screens

Preface

Globalization and technology are rapidly altering the nature of today's international business practices. The process of developing and making strategic decisions is being continuously transformed through advances in the global business environment's technological change rates, sophistication, and cross-fertilization. In the world arena, current economic, political, and technological events play a significant role in how strategies are formulated for achieving both short- and long-term goals.

When *The Global Business Game* was created, it was based on recognizing the immense challenges presented by today's fast-paced business world. Thus, using a flexible platform, a simulation was designed that could be changed as the world changed. In handling currency fluctuations, maneuvering through critical political and economic incidents, and using real economic data, students develop strategies and techniques that model situations they will encounter throughout their business careers. The result of the collaboration of a top software developer and an experienced editorial team, *The Global Business Game* is a unique simulation that takes the lead among a new millennium's strategic games.

The Global Business Game has been designed as a companion to the textbook by Michael A. Hitt, R. Duane Ireland, and Robert E. Hoskisson, *Strategic Management: Competitiveness and Globalization* (5th ed.; Cincinnati: South-Western College Publishing, 2003). It can also be used as a stand-alone game or as a core supplement for courses in strategic management, business policy, or international management at the upper-class, undergraduate, and graduate levels. *The Global Business Game* is also remarkably flexible. Game administrators are given the tools to determine the number and variety of products to be manufactured and sold and the location of company operations, to decide whether to invoke critical incidents, and to define the parameters of play. Unlike many other published games, *The Global Business Game* offers an Administrator's Manual that is straightforward and complete in all matters relating to the successful use of the simulation itself and the experiential learning method which it exemplifies.

In *The Global Business Game* students assume management of a firm that manufactures and sells television sets both directly and through wholesalers. The company is now under attack from its competitors and is faced with consumer demands for higher-quality products and features. To ensure a unique business experience for each player, the simulation has the following features:

- **Global Focus.** Competition can be conducted in countries representing the three major trade regions with their associated trade barriers and restrictions—the United States, Mexico, Germany, Spain, Japan, and Thailand.
- **Flexible Business Environment.** The game administrator decides the number and variety of products manufactured and sold, as well as the location of company operations. Choices range from a one-country, one-product operation to multiple products in six countries.
- **Multiple Strategic Choices.** Students can design and implement a full range of international business-level and functional strategies within a single-business, corporate-level strategy.
- **International Dynamics.** Players experience currency fluctuations, value-added taxes and dividend taxes, differing labor wages, and productivity/absenteeism rates within the use of exporting, technology transfers, licensing, wholly owned subsidiaries, and strategic alliances as international market entry modes.
- **Supports Windows® 95/98, NT and XP.** The game uses standard Windows® functionality, including spreadsheet models designed for Excel®use.
- **Market Research Studies.** Research studies on industry activities can be purchased in order to plan which markets to enter and to improve competitive advantage.
- **Critical Incidents.** The game administrator can invoke a number of critical incidents, which emphasize the "soft" side of the strategic manager's decision-making situation.
- **Reality-based.** Real-world economic data can be used on a quarterly basis for each country in play and for the world's major financial markets.

Today's business game is an extremely complex entity and requires a great number of talents and skills to bring it from a concept to something that is alive and usable for management education and development purposes. *The Global Business Game* is an example of how computer-based games will be designed and programmed in the future. Because of its complexity, which lies below the page and is not apparent to the game user, the list of those whose talents should be acknowledged would be formidable and interminable. Thus, for the sake of brevity, and also to honor their efforts, I will acknowledge those who have had the most direct impact on the development of *The Global Business Game*.

First and foremost, I acknowledge the help of my wife, Nancy, who has read and reread the game's written text too many times to mention. She has also served as a game assistant and creative companion in the many uses of various business games both in the United States and overseas, where my beliefs in the universality of the gaming experience were intensified.

Within business gaming circles, I must acknowledge the energy with which C. Richard Roberts served as my major co-author on many research studies on the validity of business games. Also within the academic realm, J. Bernard Keys has been very important in my associations with other gaming professionals and their academic societies. He has been at the center of the business gaming movement since the early 1970s and was kind enough to recognize and encourage my talents. In a more broad academic context, my efforts with both the Association for Business Games and Experiential Learning and the journal *Simulation & Gaming* have served as outlets for my research, as well as providing informed opinions about the nature of games and the experiential learning process.

The last individuals and groups that must be acknowledged are in the technical and academic realm. Robert Hoskisson served as liaison between myself and the Hitt, Ireland, and Hoskisson team to ensure that a more complete integration was accomplished between *The Global Business Game* and their strategic management textbook. Technical advice on many of the game's accounting and financial details was provided by Martin Kehlmann, managing partner of the accounting firm BDO Seidman, while Alfredo Mauri of Saint Joseph University's Haub School of Business and Brett Gaskill from the Stack-On Products Company served as this edition's beta-testers.

Luis Flores, Northern Illinois University, DeKalb, Illinois
Marilyn R. Kaplan, University of Texas at Dallas
Sylvain Montreuil, Université de Moncton, Moncton, New Brunswick, Canada
Olice H. Embry, Columbus State University, Columbus, Georgia
R.J. Pettersen, Central College of TAFE, Perth, Western Australia
Roland M. Porter, Lane College, Jackson, Tennessee
William Ritchie, Florida State University, Tallahassee, Florida
John Voyer, University of Southern Maine, Portland, Maine

Last, but most important, are my many students of all types and needs, who helped me learn more about how games should be designed and used. Students such as these are the only real reason this game exists, and it is their needs I hope I am filling.

South-Western/Thomson Learning assembled a very professional and thorough team, headed by John Szilagyi, Executive Editor, and together with Dan Plofchan, Production Editor; Karen Schaffer, Media Production Editor; Kristen Meere, Media Developmental Editor; Vicky True, Media Technology Editor; and Rob Bloom, Senior Marketing Manager, which has made this project a reality.

Special thanks go to Brian Makuch at Bitfoundry, who diligently and creatively provided the game's programming and coordinated the changes to this edition.

I hope that I have done justice to all of those who have helped in this project, whether mentioned here or known only to me. I have been honored by their efforts and my associations with them, and I trust this business game returns the favor.

Joseph Wolfe

Chapter

1

The Global Household Audio and Video Equipment Industry

This chapter is a general introduction to the world that has been created by *The Global Business Game*'s (GBG) model. The game itself is very flexible and provides your game administrator with a number of options regarding its complexity. Depending on the learning objectives chosen for you, your company may be competing as a manufacturer of 25-inch nationally and privately branded color television sets for sale in your home country, which might be the United States. Should your game administrator wish to give you more strategic options, your company might be allowed to increase its scope to include 27-inch sets. If your game administrator wants to present you with a challenge that has international dimensions, you might have the option of building new manufacturing facilities in Mexico, or Germany and Spain, or Japan and Thailand. Under these conditions, your company could sell the sets made in those countries throughout the world. Before your game begins, your instructor or game administrator will inform you of your particular game's configuration and will provide you with start-up information on how your firm has performed in its most recent business quarter.

The Global Business Game is a simplified model of the structure and details of the television segment of the Household Audio and Video Equipment Industry (SIC 3651200).[*] Because the GBG is a teaching simulation, it simplifies the real world, for if it duplicated reality it would take a lifetime to master! Instead, the game's model captures those elements essential to understanding how globally competitive industries operate and the options and operating methods allowed firms in such industries. It gives you a chance to practice strategic management and to better understand your own strengths and weaknesses as a key business decision maker. Since many companies and industries now compete at the international level, even the strongest domestic firms are no longer protected from foreign competition. Such factors as fast, inexpensive communications, rising income levels in numerous countries, and the internationalization of consumer tastes and expectations have created world markets for a large array of goods and products. For financial survival, at the minimum, or financial security and growth, at the maximum, companies must be able to handle competition on the international level. The GBG has been created to help you become more attuned to this competitive world.

Because this is a global industry, many different-sized companies manufacture and sell their products across national borders; these products are as diverse as juke boxes, microphones, television sets, and remote control devices. Your company's previous management group in *The Global Business Game* has chosen to pursue a single-business, corporate-level strategy by competing in a smaller segment of the household audio and video equipment industry. Considering your firm's more limited assets, as well as its specialized competencies, it chose specifically to manufacture and sell through wholesale distributors a limited line of middle-sized consumer-related television sets (SIC 3651200)— after having used an unrelated or conglomerate corporate-level strategy when it ventured in small clock radios, record turntables, and audio tape recorders and players.

---

[*]The *Standard Industrial Classification Manual* describes this industry as "Establishments primarily engaged in manufacturing electronic audio and video equipment for home entertainment (including automotive), such as television sets, radio broadcast receivers, tape players, phonographs, and video recorders and players. This industry also includes establishments primarily engaged in manufacturing public address systems and music distribution apparatus." See *Standard Industrial Classification Manual* (Springfield, Va.: National Technical Information Service, 1987), p. 228.

INDUSTRY DEMAND AND PRODUCT CHARACTERISTICS

The demand for television sets depends on a number of intertwined factors, both economic and socioeconomic in nature. These factors include disposable incomes and literacy levels, the country's degree of electrification, leisure time and how it is used by the population, the relative costs of alternative pastimes and diversions, and the population's size and number of household units.

The set you are making is the result of a series of inventions and discoveries that began in Britain in 1908, when Campbell-Swinton proved that light signals could be transmitted and received by a cathode-ray tube. In 1920, John Logie Baird demonstrated "radio-vision" in London. Four years later he presented his transmitting and receiving system at the Wembley Exhibition. It was a mechanical system using synchronized spinning disks. Britain was the first country to have regular television service, which was begun by the BBC in November 1936 from a London hilltop.

Although the British were at the vanguard regarding television's basic technological research, it was in the United States that its commercial possibilities and mass market appeal were the most thoroughly exploited. Applied research was directed by RCA's Director of Electronic Research V. K. Zworykin in the early 1930s. RCA invented the iconoscope (the part of the camera for capturing broadcasted images) and then the kinescope for viewing the images. By the late 1940s, television stations were operating in most of America's larger cities, although viewing hours were restricted.

Although many black-and-white television sets were being purchased by American consumers at the time, color television set demonstrations were also occurring. The CBS network's field sequential system of spinning colored disks initially challenged RCA and its NBC network for supremacy, but the latter's more complicated but theoretically superior three-color gun system prevailed. Today almost all new television sets are color sets, and all come with a number of convenience features.

The most popular-size sets in North America are those with picture tubes measuring 25 or 27 inches diagonally across the face. These sets lie between the industry's smallest 19- and 20-inch model, and its big-screen models, measuring 31 inches or more. In the United States, the industry's 25-inch TVs are often used as secondary or even tertiary sets in larger bedrooms or dens. The big-screen sets are used in large family rooms. Monophonic 25-inch sets retail in the United States for $250 to $280, with those featuring stereophonic or "surround" sound retailing for $270 to $350. This class of sets, which is presented in Exhibit 1.1, is limited regarding the number of features and amenities.

In contrast, the industry's 27-inch sets offer higher-quality sound and a host of useful features and enhancements. Many provide color-"warmth" adjustments that present flesh tones and interiors in a more favorable light, automatic volume controls that tone down loud advertisements, S-video-input jacks that take advantage of the superior picture quality generated by Hi8 or S-VHS-C camcorders, picture-in-picture, and audio circuitry that emulates surround sound. Exhibit 1.1 cites the typical features of sets in this size category. These television sets currently retail for $350 to $580 in the United States, but have higher price tags in foreign markets due to the tariffs and value-added taxes (VATs) often levied on them. They are also retailed through relatively inefficient marketing channels.

Sets of these two sizes generally produce acceptable pictures and sound. There are substantial differences, however, in the reliability of the various brands in the marketplace. Many consumers attach great importance to having a

Exhibit 1.1   25- and 27-Inch Sets

25-Inch Set Features	27-Inch Features	
Remote control	Universal remote control	Ambient sound
On-screen multilingual menu	"Warmth" adjustment	Audio-output jacks
Closed-caption capability	Automatic Volume control	Commercial-skip timer
Closed captioning when muted	S-video-input jack	Picture-in-picture
Stereo	Multiple-input jacks	Channel block-out
Commercial-skip timer	On-screen multilingual menu	12-month parts warranty
Separate audio program	Closed-caption capability	24-month picture-tube warranty
12-month parts warranty	Closed-captioning when muted	Stereo
24-month picture-tube warranty		

Exhibit 1.2   25-inch and 27-inch Repairs and Serious Problems by Manufacturer

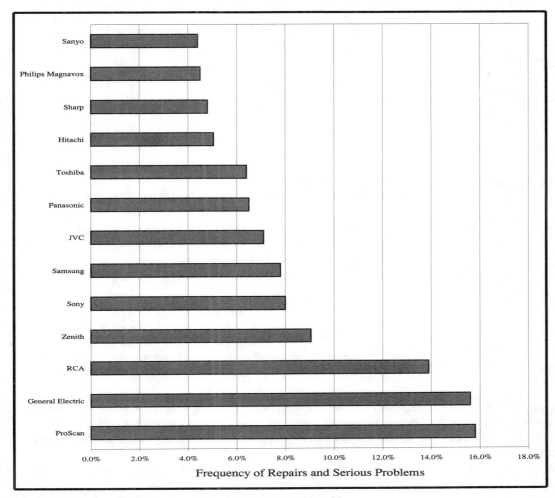

Source: Repair History: TVs, Consumer Reports, December, 2000, p. 27.

set not prone to breakdowns. Exhibit 1.2 presents the five-year frequency of repair records associated with many of the world's major television brands.

The demand for these features, and the ability to pay for them, differ among countries. The number of broadcast television channels and cable channels also varies dramatically from country to country. Additionally, the television set's use as a home entertainment medium varies depending upon the household's financial circumstances. Various features are also more or less attractive due to differing literacy levels, the availability of repair facilities, and the product's life-cycle stage within each country. Depending on the situation, increased complexity or greater product sophistication could be a product disadvantage. Exhibit 1.3 (page 4) shows that a high degree of product saturation and market maturity exists in the United States for television sets. The markets of Spain, Mexico, and Thailand are relatively unsaturated in this regard.

WORLD AND NATIONAL MARKETS

Because the household audio and video equipment industry is global in scope, competitors must systematically monitor many global economic trends and developments. Raw population projections, such as those shown in Exhibit 1.4,

Exhibit 1.3 Television Set Ownership in the United States

Item	1970	1980	1995	1996	1997	1998
Percent of households	95.3	97.9	98.3	98.3	98.4	98.3
Sets in homes (millions)	81.0	128.0	217.0	223.0	229.0	235.0
Sets per home	1.4	1.7	2.3	2.3	2.4	2.4
Color set households (millions)	21.0	63.0	94.0	95.0	97.0	98.0

Source: U.S. Bureau of the Census, Statistical Abstract of the United States: 2000 (Washington, DC: U.S. Government Printing Office), 2000, Table 910.

Exhibit 1.4 Major Region Population Projections (in millions)

Major Region	Year			Growth (in percent)
	2000	2025	2050	
Asia	3,688.1	4,765.7	5,368.5	45.6
Africa	805.2	1,273.3	1,845.7	129.2
Europe	729.0	714.3	642.4	−11.9
South America	346.5	435.6	480.3	38.6
North America	480.5	611.9	722.3	50.3
Oceania	30.8	39.9	45.0	46.1
World	6,080.1	7,840.7	9,104.2	49.7

Source: World Almanac & Book of Facts, 2001 (Mahwah, NJ: World Almanac Books, 2001), p. 862.

indicate that the world's population will increase about 49.7 percent in the very long term. This results in a 1.0 percent average annual increase in the number of people who might potentially watch a television set. The greatest growth will be found in the developing areas of Asia, Africa, and Oceania as well as in the more highly developed North America due to immigration.

Although the gross estimates for these areas are notable, your company's previous management group has been relatively uninterested in conducting international operations and has focused solely on its home country of the United States. Some in your company, however, are aware of international developments, especially the profits that might be gained through expanded operations encouraged in North America by North American Free Trade Agreement (NAFTA) and in Western Europe and Asia via their respective trading zones of the European Union (EU) and the Asia Pacific Economic Cooperation (APEC). Exhibit 1.5 shows the projected population growth rates for these economic zones and for the specific countries possibly available to you in *The Global Business Game*.

Exhibit 1.5 Population Projections for Selected NAFTA, EU, and APEC Countries (in millions)

Country	Year			Growth (in percent)
	2000	2025	2050	
United States	275.6	335.4	394.2	43.0
Mexico	100.4	141.6	167.5	66.8
Germany	82.8	75.4	57.4	-30.7
Spain	40.0	36.8	29.4	-26.5
Japan	126.6	119.9	101.3	-20.0
Thailand	61.2	70.3	69.7	13.9

Source: World Almanac & Book of Facts, 2001 (Mahwah, NJ: World Almanac Books, 2001), pp. 861–862.

While a country's population growth is important when seeking foreign markets, your company was also interested in the buying power of each nation's population as well as its current stock of television sets. Exhibit 1.6 displays each nation's television set ownership in 2000. On a per capita basis, a relatively low level of television set saturation has been realized in Thailand and Mexico, with a modest degree in Germany and Spain. The Japanese and American markets have reached the saturation point, with all new sales being based on replacement demand.

Exhibit 1.6   Television Sets in Use, 2000

Country	Sets
United States	222,103,514.4
Mexico	27,295,136.4
Germany	46,949,130.3
Spain	16,358,638.4
Japan	86,813,283.5
Thailand	15,552,642.0

Source: Derived from population statistics in the *World Almanac & Book of Facts, 2001* (Mahwah, NJ: World Almanac Books, 2001), and set-use rates in U.S. Census Bureau, *Statistical Abstract of the United States: 2000* (Washington, DC: U.S. Government Printing Office, 2001).

To create their best estimates of each nation's attractiveness as a site for further expansion, your company's previous management group consolidated its thinking in the graphic form presented in Exhibit 1.7 (page 6). The size of the circles indicates each country's relative buying power. Market attractiveness is an index of subjective feelings about the ease of doing business in each country.

Your company's research into various new markets and manufacturing sites produced a portfolio reflecting certain macroeconomic features for six countries that were considered likely expansion candidates.

Germany. The reunification of the Federal Republic of Germany (West Germany) with the German Democratic Republic (East Germany) on October 2–3, 1990, created an economic unit now numbering over 82 million people. As the European Community has taken shape, Germany has assumed a central role in its affairs as well as the euro's value. A low internal inflation rate and elaborate rail, roadway, and telephone infrastructures along with a pro-business governmental posture make this country an attractive economic opportunity despite its long-term projected population decline. Its per capita income, while not as great as that found in the Scandinavian countries, is the highest in Europe after Denmark. Its major industries are steel, ships, vehicles, machinery, coal, and chemicals. About 34 percent of its labor force is engaged in industry and commerce, and 64 percent in various service industries. Less positive features are labor rates that are the highest in the world—the equivalent of $27.20 per hour in the early 2000s—a work week of thirty-five hours plus vacations lasting up to six weeks, and highly participative unions.

Key statistics for Germany in early 2000:

Major cities—Berlin (3.5 million), Hamburg (1.7 million), Munich (1.2 million), Cologne (1.0 million), Essen (0.6 million), and Frankfurt (0.6 million)
Chief ports—Hamburg, Bremen, Bremerhaven, Lubeck, and Rostock
Population density—601 per square mile
Land mass—137,800 square miles
Literacy rate—100 percent, with compulsory education for ages 6 to 15
Daily newspaper circulation—311 per 1,000 population
Airports—35
Physicians—1 per 290 persons
Hospital beds—1 per 138 persons
Infant mortality—5.08 per 1,000 births

Exhibit 1.7   Country Market Size, Growth and Attractiveness

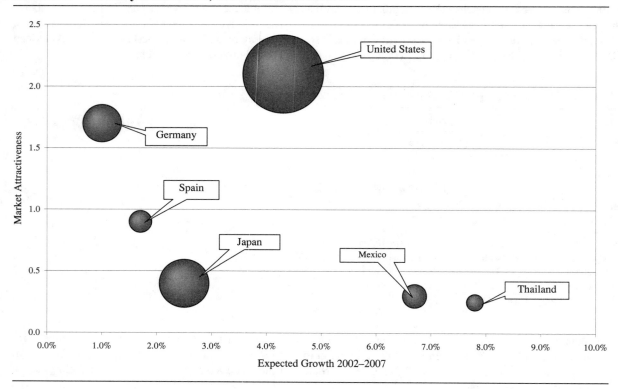

Spain. This country continues to be a favorite manufacturing site for European firms wishing to lower their labor costs. The economy has been growing at a relatively high rate for the past several years, although it also has a very high unemployment rate. Despite this level of unemployment, wages have been rising, and they have been outgaining increases in worker productivity. Spain has had rather turbulent politics, and a degree of political unrest lingers. A 1981 coup was foiled by King Juan Carlos, and the Socialist Workers' Party under Feleipe Gonzalez Marquez won four consecutive general elections from 1982 to 1993. He lost to a coalition of conservative and regional parties in March 1996. Basque separatist activities continue after they cancelled their September 1998 cease fire in November 1999. Both Catalonia and the Basque country have been granted autonomy.

Key statistics for Spain in early 2000:

Major cities—Madrid (4.1 million), Barcelona (2.8 million), Valencia (0.8 million), Sevilla (0.7 million), and
    Zaragoza (0.6 million)
Major ports—Barcelona, Bilbao, Valencia, and Cartagena
Population density—205 per square mile
Land mass—194.9 square miles
Literacy rate—97 percent, with 10 years of compulsory education
Newspaper circulation—99 per 1,000 population
Airports—25
Physicians—1 per 241 persons
Hospital beds—1 per 234 persons
Infant mortality—6.31 per 1,000 births

Mexico. This country's economic and political history has been turbulent and long-lasting. Various administrations have attempted to improve the population's welfare through economic and social reforms, but little real progress has been made. The Institutional Revolutionary Party (PRI) dominated politics from 1929 until the late 1990, when it was defeated by Vicente Fox Quesada on July 2, 2000. Zapatista National Liberation Army guerrillas launched a southern Mexico uprising on January 1, 1994. The peso was devalued in the 1980s, and an austerity plan and aid from the United States saved the country's currency from collapsing again in early 1995. It has been estimated that an amount almost 40 percent as large as Mexico's official GDP is obtained through illegal or undocumented activities. Despite having one of the hemisphere's lowest factory labor rates (at about $1.83 an hour), much unemployment and under-employment exists.

Key statistics for Mexico in early 2000:

Major cities—Mexico City (8.5 million), Guadalajara (1.6 million), and Puebla (1.2 million)
Major ports—Coatzacoalcos, Mazatlan, Tampico, and Veracruz
Population density—132 per square mile
Land mass—761,600 square miles
Literacy rate—90 percent, with 10 years of compulsory education
Newspaper circulation—97 per 1,000 population
Airports—83
Physicians—1 per 613 persons
Hospital beds—1 per 1,196 persons
Infant mortality—23.4 per 1,000 births

Japan. "Japan, Inc." is no longer the economic juggernaut it once was. Legend has it the Japanese empire was founded by Jimmu in 660 B.C. China has had a great influence on Japan's civilization and it carried out expansionist dreams through wars with China, Russia, and Germany, culminating in its attack on the United States at Pearl Harbor in 1941. After World War II, it rebuilt itself through close and protective relations between government and business and a manufacturing base built on efficiency and productivity. Although still the world's second-largest economy, it has been mired in recession since 1998, with much needed reform in its banking sector constantly being delayed. Reform candidate Junichiro Koizumi was swept into power in April 2001 with the expectation that it would take three years for his reforms to take effect. Relations with the United States have been strained since President George W. Bush rebuked the Kyoto Accord on global warming while the public has continued pressure on the U.S. to abandon its military base on Okinawa.

Key statistics for Japan in early 2000:

Major cities—Tokyo (8.0 million), Osaka (2.6 million), Nagoya (2.2 million), Sapporo (1.8 million), and Kyoto (1.5 million)
Major ports—Tokyo, Kobe, Osaka, Nagoya, Chiba, Kawasaki, and Hakodate
Population density—867 per square mile
Land mass—145,882 square miles
Literacy rate—100 percent
Airports—73
Physicians—1 per 522 persons
Hospital beds—1 per 74 persons
Infant mortality—4.1 per 1,000 births

Thailand. An economic collapse of the Pacific Rim countries was precipitated by this country's devaluation of its currency in July 1997. In August Thailand received $15.0 billion in international emergency loans. The crisis continued despite the creation of a new constituion in September. Its economy has never been very robust, and the corruption that has traditionally existed in high places has made it especially difficult for the government to take effective action. The country has also been wracked with an AIDS epidemic since the mid-1990s. The United Nations estimates that in 1999 more than 750,000 people had HIV/AIDS.

Key statistics for Thailand in early 2000:

Major cities—Bangkok (7.3 million), Nakhon Ratchasima (0.2 million), Chiang Mai (0.2 million), and Hat Yai (0.2 million)
Major ports—Bangkok and Sattahip

Population density—308 per square mile
Land mass—198,500 square miles
Literacy rate—94 percent, compulsory for those ages 6 to 15
Newspaper circulation—63 per 1,000 population
Airports—25
Physicians—1 per 3,461 persons
Hospital beds—1 per 599 persons
Infant mortality—28.3 per 1,000 births

United States. Once incomparable in most economic activities, this country's businesses have encountered strong competition on their home soil, while finding it difficult to sell many of their products overseas. Despite these problems, the United States is both the world's richest and largest market and one whose government is basically pro-business. Its relatively low interest and inflation rates have led to the longest run of GDP growth in its history although an economic slowdown occurred in mid-2001. Because of its relatively high manufacturing labor costs (at about $18.58 per hour), a number of its major corporations have established offshore operations. The dollar has been strong against most Asian currencies as well as the euro.

Key statistics for the United States in early 2000:

Major cities—New York City (7.4 million), Los Angeles (3.4 million), Chicago (3.1 million), Houston (1.7 million),
    and Philadelphia (1.6 million)
Population density—74 per square mile
Land mass—3,717,796 square miles
Literacy rate—97 percent, with compulsory education for ages 7 to 16
Newspaper circulation—215 per 1,000 population
Airports—834
Physicians—1 per 365 persons
Hospital beds—1 per 243 persons
Infant mortality—6.7 per 1,000 births

COUNTRY SEASONAL DEMAND

Your company has also collected information on past television set sales by nation. In gathering data, it became clear that television set sales varied throughout the year regardless of each country's underlying macroeconomic elements, and that seasonal variation differed from country to country. In the United States, your television sets (because of their size) have proven to be good Christmas gifts for a child's bedroom. In Germany and Spain, two countries that have many rabid soccer fans, television set sales spike in June shortly before the World Cup matches begin.

The empirically derived seasonal indicators your management group has created are presented in Exhibit 1.8. These indexes, because they are based on long-term, relatively constant factors, will not change over the course of your simulation. They also reflect the fact that distributors stock their warehouses well before retailers stock their shelves with television sets in anticipation of consumer demand.

Exhibit 1.8   Television Set Seasonal Indexes by Quarter

Country	Quarter 1	Quarter 2	Quarter 3	Quarter 4
United States	.74	.82	1.31	1.13
Mexico	1.21	1.11	.81	.87
Germany	1.17	1.08	.83	.92
Spain	1.19	1.10	.79	.92
Japan	.84	1.00	1.12	1.04
Thailand	.94	1.02	1.03	1.01

COMPETITIVE STRATEGIES IN GLOBAL INDUSTRIES

A global industry can be defined as one in which participants are present in all key international markets, demand for the product is standardized and the product itself is fairly standardized, and a significant portion of the product's components or raw materials are obtained from international sources. Accordingly, the automobile industry is a global industry. This could also be said of the tire, watch, and pharmaceutical industries.

Because of the growing importance of global competitiveness, various authors have attempted to describe the basic strategies that can be employed by companies competing in them. It has been suggested that four competitive strategies exist in global industries: broad-line global competition, global focus, national focus, and protected niche. This matrix of strategies has been expanded to include a strategy of integrated low-cost/differentiation in global markets.

The television set industry is involved in global international competition. A firm thus needs to employ international business-level strategies to enter the international markets and market segments available. In determining how your company should compete in *The Global Business Game,* the strategies that have been used in the real world can be used, to some degree, in the game you are about to play. These business-level strategies, and how they can be implemented in the game, are the following:

- International low-cost strategy—Create low-cost operations in your firm's home country and export standardized products to target markets using foreign-owned distribution channels.
- International differentiation strategy—Create unique products and company-owned distribution channels in each foreign market.
- International focus strategy—Within each foreign market, limit production to the single set size, quality grade, and channel support activities associated with a particular customer segment.
- International integrated low-cost/differentiation strategy—Obtain low manufacturing costs by building factories in low labor cost countries, or by using automation to lower overall unit manufacturing while indicating product differences through sales promotion efforts.

Because your firm may choose to enter a number of country markets, its international corporate strategy can take one of three forms. If your corporate-level strategy is multidomestic, you would decentralize your management team's talents to the country unit level. Within each country unit, the country unit manager would decide the appropriate price, quality level, segment, and service level based on local competitive conditions. Under a global corporate-level strategy, decisions would be highly centralized and controlled, with standardized products being made and shipped to all country units. If your firm chose a transnational strategy, it would try to achieve both global efficiency and local responsiveness. It could do this by manufacturing a fairly universal, standardized product in a low labor cost country while tailoring its sales promotion tactics and appeals to local tastes.

While both international business-level and corporate-level strategic decisions must be made, you will have to implement those strategies through your market entry method. The market entry modes available to you in *The Global Business Game* are exporting, licensing/strategic alliances, and new, wholly owned subsidiaries. Under the exporting market entry mode, your firm merely ships goods from its home country factory to the chosen country unit(s). This mode may require expansion of your domestic factory's capacity and it will be attended by inflexible shipping arrangements, tariff restrictions, and shipping charges. Under the licensing/strategic alliances mode, your firm can have a country unit competitor manufacture television sets for you while sharing in research and development costs on patent-pursuing activities. Using a wholly owned subsidiary market entry method is costly, but allows for the greatest level of control. This mode would be implemented through building a correct-size factory in the country unit while simultaneously creating a company-owned wholesaling operation.

In choosing which corporate-level, business-level, and market entry strategy to implement, you should consider a number of factors: the internal resources possessed by your management team, the physical and financial resources your company has at this time and can make available to itself, and the global opportunities available to all companies in your industry. A number of experiential exercises have been created to help you through the process of auditing your firm's current situation, and then structuring your group so that you can proceed in an intelligent manner in choosing and implementing your company's strategic intent. This Web site contains these materials under "Player Resources" at the following address: http://www.swcollege.com/management/gbg/gbg.html.

Chapter 2

Company History and Background

The company you will be running was born of the enthusiasm of Gary Elliott, Arthur Moore, David Stevenson, and Casimir (Casey) Sobieski. They had served together in the Signal Corps during World War II, but had previously been employed as electronics engineers at RCA's David Sarnoff Laboratories. The work they performed there was the basic research that made television commercially feasible. Because they were avid tinkerers and experimenters with everything that went into that era's electronic gear, they dreamed of starting their own home electronics firm once the war was over.

By early 1948, after mustering out of the Signal Corps, they had accumulated enough private capital to start making products, but ones that did not require large amounts of start-up monies. Although they yearned to get into making television sets, they first turned their attention to making the more easily assembled FM radios and wire recorders that were just being introduced in the United States.

Their first television set was a very small unit introduced in 1954. It was given the brand name MagnaArgus. The MagnaArgus had a 10-inch picture tube with an 8 5/8 × 6 1/4-inch screen. It retailed for $275. The company's picture tubes were purchased under a RCA licensing agreement; the sets were hand-assembled in a small plant in Erie, Pennsylvania. The sets sold well in regional markets in western New York and northern Ohio, but limited quantities of picture tubes and quality assurance problems kept the partners from expanding their sales territory.

A number of successor models were produced, and the company had visions of becoming a national brand. As the 1960s wore on, however, the company's founders were unable to broaden the firm's product line of television sets and had to fall back on the production of high-fidelity equipment and FM tuners as a way of stabilizing their earnings. More important, a number of domestic television set manufacturers were being squeezed out of existence, and by the early 1970s foreign manufacturers from the Pacific Rim had entered the industry and were making great headway with their reliable yet moderately priced offerings. Your company's market position and economic fortunes began to deteriorate, and its founders decided to go public in 1985 under the corporate name MagnaArgus, Inc. This was done to obtain enough new capital to either grow—or die—by becoming a niche television set manufacturer.

With its new capital, and an expanded board of directors and shareholder interests to consider, your firm took a number of years to implement its new strategy of focused efforts. Its high-fidelity equipment products were pulled from the market, and new specialty dealers and wholesalers had to be enlisted. Most important, its Erie, Pennsylvania, production operations had to be converted to full-time television set manufacturing, albeit at a very flexible level of operations, given a lack of knowledge of the scale of operations the company could attain as a niche player.

Your firm was often in a precarious situation, but it has survived and has generated modest but unstable profits. Its founders have long since given up active management of the company, and in fact, three of them have died—after transferring their shareholdings to their children, who have pursued other interests. Knowing that their children had no interest in running your company, Gary, Arthur, David, and Casey had actively hired and groomed new managers as their replacements. You are now the newest generation of their management team, and they have placed their legacy in your hands.

In anticipation of future, possible global growth, as well as hoping to ensure the company's survival, Gary Elliott, as your firm's last active co-founding manager, asked your company's accounting firm to create an accounting system that would handle most eventualities. Your accounting firm complied and prepared mock-ups of the types of reports the new system would produce if all possible company operations were implemented.

Because your company was operating only in your home country of the United States when the mock-ups were created, only the income statements, balance sheets, and industry reports for the United States are described in depth. Should your game administrator choose a different home country and additional market areas for your simulation, the start-up reports provided at the beginning of play would reflect that change. Your game administrator will also inform you before play begins of the range of different-size television sets you will be able to sell and the markets and countries in which you will be allowed to compete. Appropriate computer-generated reports will be provided for these conditions. At this juncture the reports for each additional market area and country in which your company decides to operate are basically the same as your North American or NAFTA report, except that all monetary values are stated in the relevant country currencies. Your consolidated corporate-level report gathers together the reports generated by each country's operation.

In *The Global Business Game* you will be interacting with the game via programs that control the game's interface. For each quarter or decision round you will submit a set of decisions that will be processed by your game administrator. Your management team will enter its decisions via GBGPlayer, which is a data entry and retrieval program found on the CD included in this manual. The decisions made by the company being demonstrated are for a company engaged only in domestic operations in the United States. Your game administrator or instructor may have you play a game where your home country may be Japan, Mexico, or Germany and you may be restricted as to the scope of brands that can be offered for sale. Regardless of the nature of your actual competitive environment, the following describes the nature of each piece of information the simulation provides players.

GLOBAL INDUSTRY REPORT

This report is received by all companies in your industry. The report displays information commonly known by companies in a real-world industry, and you can assume the information presented is as accurate as possible.

GLOBAL INDUSTRY A REPORT—These two lines designate the industry to which your company has been assigned. Your game administrator may create a number of independently operating industries. Your company's performance will be judged only against the performance of the other firms in your own industry.

YEAR 2002—This indicates the simulation's operating year. Your game administrator will inform you of the number of years your game will entail.

QUARTER 4—This part of the line identifies the simulation's operating quarter. Your game administrator will inform you about the number of quarters the simulation will run. Quarter 4 would be the business year's fourth quarter while, for example, YEAR 2003, QUARTER 2 would be the second quarter of the year 2003.

WAGE RATES—The average wage, in local currency values, of workers that can be assigned to assembling 25-inch and 27-inch sets.

SHORT-TERM RATE—The general interest rates found for ninety-day loans in each market area's major financial markets of New York City, Frankfurt, and Tokyo. This is an indicator of the interest rate a country operation would have to pay for a ninety-day short-term loan given the country unit's credit rating.

BOND RATE—A statement of the general yield rates found for ten-year bonds in each market area's major financial markets of New York City, Frankfurt, and Tokyo. This is an indicator of the nominal interest rate a country operation would have to pay for a ten-year callable bond given the country unit's credit rating. This bond rate serves as the basis of your firm's effective interest rate on its twenty-year bonds.

STOCK MARKET INDEX—The stock market indexes associated with each market area's financial center. For North America this is the Dow Jones Industrial Average (DJIA), for Western Europe it is the Frankfurt DAX-30, and for Asia it is Tokyo's Nikkei 225. These indexes may be updated throughout the simulation and can be found via the Internet or in any of the commonly available financial newspapers, such as the *Wall Street Journal*'s section C.

GDP YEAR/QUARTER—Each relevant country's quarterly gross domestic product changes are reported as index numbers based on the year 2002 for the current year and operating quarter and its predicted value for the following quarter and four quarters after the game's start-up year. The values presented here reflect either real-world data or numbers created by your game administrator to reflect comparative growth rates between the economies being simulated.

SUBASSEMBLIES—The lot price of the group 1 and group 2 subassemblies by grade needed for the manufacture of each television set, free on board (FOB) Hong Kong. Subassemblies are purchased in lots of 100, and their prices may vary throughout the simulation's run.

Global Industry A Report
Year 2002 Quarter 4

	US$ U.S.
Wage Rates:	
25" TV	17.56
27" TV	17.74
Short-Term Rate	5.71%
Bond Rate	9.01%
Stock Market Index	10067.86
GDP Q4 2002	100.00
GDP Q1 2003	100.00
GDP Q4 2003	100.23

Subassemblies	Grade A	Grade B	Grade C
Group 1			
Group 2			

Bulletin

The Home Elec
bids for its Kin
quarter. The w
Index at or abo
25" TVs 1,6
27" TVs 3,0

Global Industry A Report
Year 2002 Quarter 4

Currency Cross Rates

	U.S.	Mexico	Japan	Thailand	EU
Dollar	1.0000	9.4650	127.3800	39.9200	0.9334
Peso	0.1057	1.0000	13.4580	4.2176	0.0986
Yen	0.0079	0.0743	1.0000	0.3134	0.0073
Baht	0.0251	0.2371	3.1909	1.0000	0.0234
Euro	1.0714	10.1403	136.4688	42.7684	1.0000

Global Industry A Report
Year 2002 Quarter 4

Firm Summaries

Firm 1 - MagnaArgus Corporation

	US$ U.S.
25" TV:	
List Price	105.00
Actual Price	102.83
27" TV:	
List Price	123.00
Actual Price	122.40

Firm 2 - Global Megapolis, Corp.

	US$ U.S.
25" TV:	
List Price	105.00
Actual Price	102.83
27" TV:	
List Price	123.00
Actual Price	122.40
Contract Bid	
25" TV	0.00

Global Industry A Report

Year 2002 Quarter 4

Consolidated Performance Indicators

Firm	US$ Profit	ROA	E.P.S	ROE	US$ Stock Price	Perform. Index
1 - MagnaArgus Corporation	-18,038	-0.21%	-0.007	-0.24%	18.55	1.00
2 - Global Megapolis, Corp.	-18,038	-0.21%	-0.007	-0.24%	18.55	1.00
3 - Consumer Electronics, Inc.	-18,038	-0.21%	-0.007	-0.24%	18.55	1.00
4 - Voltavision Company	-18,038	-0.21%	-0.007	-0.24%	18.55	1.00

BULLETIN BOARD—A listing of various events or announcements associated with your simulation. Your game administrator may present critical incidents for you to solve and bids and offers for used automatons. Home Electronics King's requests for bids on privately labeled sets will be found here. Periodic announcements of new product patents obtained, fines and penalties assessed, and factory openings and expansions will also be found on the bulletin board. The value of any construction announced in the bulletin board covers only the plant's line worker capacity and not the value of any automatons that may be installed in the factory or the cost of the land needed by the plant. The true value of any new capacity is reported in the country unit's balance sheet, but this is confidential information.

CURRENCY CROSS RATES—Displays the currency exchange rates in effect during the decision quarter. These rates will change from quarter to quarter.

GLOBAL INDUSTRY A REPORT—This information is presented to all firms in your industry. Your industry will begin with between three and nine companies competing against each other.

25″ TV LIST PRICE—Each company's list price to wholesalers for its 25-inch television sets in the countries listed.

25″ TV ACTUAL PRICE—A fairly accurate estimate of the actual market price wholesalers paid for 25-inch sets in the previous quarter. This price reflects trade discounts and price incentives employed by each firm to induce greater sales of their 25-inch television sets in the countries listed.

27″ TV LIST PRICE—The company's list price to wholesalers for its 27-inch television sets in the countries listed.

27″ TV ACTUAL PRICE—A somewhat accurate estimate of the actual price wholesalers paid for the designated product in the previous quarter. This price reflects trade discounts and price incentives used to further stimulate sales of its 27-inch television sets in the countries listed.

25″ TV CONTRACT BID—A fairly accurate estimate of the unit price charged for 25-inch sets as either a product for private-label purposes or for contract sales to another firm. If both private-label contracts and manufacturing-contract sales were made, this is the weighted price of those two sales.

27″ TV CONTRACT BID—A fairly accurate estimate of the unit price charged for 27-inch television sets as either a product for private-label purposes or for contract sales to another firm. If both private-label contracts and manufacturing-contract sales were made, this is the weighted price of those two sales.

SALES OFFICES—The number of sales offices operated by the company exclusive of those attached to its distribution center(s) and factories.

DISTRIBUTION CENTERS—The number of regional distribution centers in operation by country. The number reported here does not reflect the distribution center that is part of any factory in the country.

C-WHOLESALERS—The number of company-owned wholesalers in operation by country.

I-WHOLESALERS—The number of independent wholesalers being employed by country.

SALES REPS—The number of sales representatives the company had in the field in each country at the end of the quarter.

CONSOLIDATED PERFORMANCE INDICATORS—A report on the economic performance of all companies in your industry at the consolidated or corporate level. The measures used are common criteria of overall organizational effectiveness. Your game administrator may use any or all these indicators. If the indicators shown here are employed, they may be weighted at the game administrator's discretion and you will be informed of the weighting scheme being employed.

PROFIT—The company's total earnings or profit for the quarter in the home country's currency unit.

ROA—The company's rate of return on assets for the quarter. This is the firm's earnings for the quarter divided by the firm's assets for the quarter.

EPS— The company's earnings per share for the quarter. This is the firm's owners' equity divided by the number of shares outstanding at the quarter's end.

ROE—The company's rate of return on owners' equity for the quarter. This is the firm's earnings for the quarter divided by the quarter's ending owners' equity (common stock, paid-in capital, current earnings plus retained earnings).

STOCK PRICE—The firm's stock price at the quarter's end.

PERFORMANCE INDEX—The weighted ranked average of the quarter's performance indicators as chosen by your game administrator.

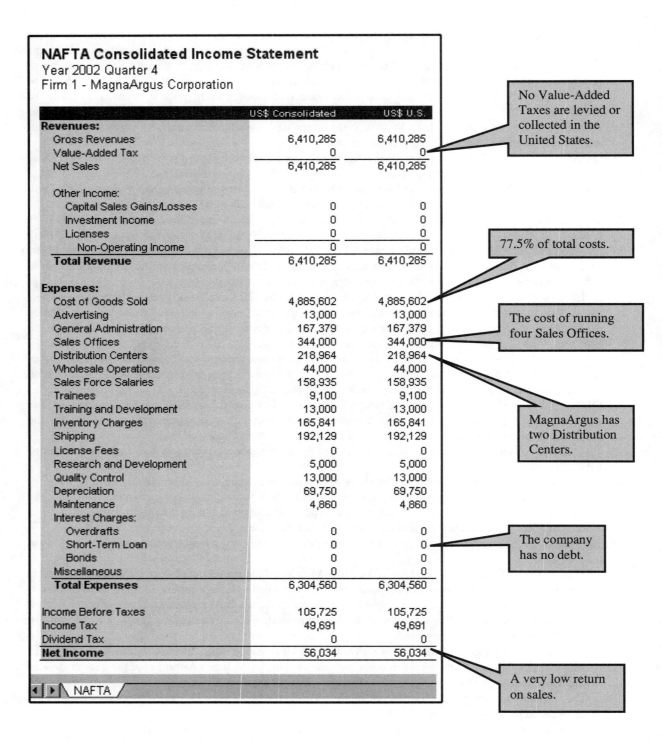

NAFTA Consolidated Income Statement
Year 2002 Quarter 4
Firm 1 - MagnaArgus Corporation

	US$ Consolidated	US$ U.S.
Revenues:		
Gross Revenues	6,410,285	6,410,285
Value-Added Tax	0	0
Net Sales	6,410,285	6,410,285
Other Income:		
Capital Sales Gains/Losses	0	0
Investment Income	0	0
Licenses	0	0
Non-Operating Income	0	0
Total Revenue	6,410,285	6,410,285
Expenses:		
Cost of Goods Sold	4,885,602	4,885,602
Advertising	13,000	13,000
General Administration	167,379	167,379
Sales Offices	344,000	344,000
Distribution Centers	218,964	218,964
Wholesale Operations	44,000	44,000
Sales Force Salaries	158,935	158,935
Trainees	9,100	9,100
Training and Development	13,000	13,000
Inventory Charges	165,841	165,841
Shipping	192,129	192,129
License Fees	0	0
Research and Development	5,000	5,000
Quality Control	13,000	13,000
Depreciation	69,750	69,750
Maintenance	4,860	4,860
Interest Charges:		
Overdrafts	0	0
Short-Term Loan	0	0
Bonds	0	0
Miscellaneous	0	0
Total Expenses	6,304,560	6,304,560
Income Before Taxes	105,725	105,725
Income Tax	49,691	49,691
Dividend Tax	0	0
Net Income	56,034	56,034

◄ | ► \ NAFTA /

Callouts:

No Value-Added Taxes are levied or collected in the United States.

77.5% of total costs.

The cost of running four Sales Offices.

MagnaArgus has two Distribution Centers.

The company has no debt.

A very low return on sales.

MARKET/COUNTRY AREA REPORTS

The next set of reports contains material that is unique and confidential to your own company's operations. Assuming your home country is the United States, you would receive balance sheets, income statements, and operating reports only for NAFTA or North American operations, and then only for U.S. operations, but not for Mexico, which operates within NAFTA, unless Mexico has been made available for commerce by your game administrator. If your company is allowed to enter any of the other market areas available in the simulation, such as APEC or EU, you would receive similar reports for the particular market areas and countries involved.

NAFTA CONSOLIDATED INCOME STATEMENT—A line identifying the market area's operations. Identical sheets are supplied for the APEC and EU market areas. Because the United States is your home country in this example, the results obtained in other countries and market areas "consolidate" U.S. operations.

FIRM 1 MAGNAARGUS CORPORATION—Your company's firm number and name. Your game administrator will assign you a company number, but you will create your firm's name before the game's start-up quarter when you initialize your company. Instructions for doing this are presented in Chapter 6.

YEAR 2002 QUARTER 4—A line indicating the simulation's operating year and quarter.

GROSS REVENUES—All revenues associated with the sale of your company's television sets. If the country in which the sale was made levies a value-added tax (VAT) or imposes a tariff on the firm's products, these taxes are included in the firm's gross revenues. This amount includes currently generated sales as well as any back orders filled from the previous operating quarter. It is possible that your sales representatives will write more orders than can be supplied from either your company's current production or finished goods inventories. Should this occur, your firm's shipping clerk allocates any available units according to the following priorities. The first priority will be product contract sales to other firms in your industry. The second priority will be contract sales obtained for private-brand purposes. The third priority will be the filling of back orders, unless you have lowered your firm's actual price for that product. If the actual price has been lowered, the back orders for that product will be cancelled at the original price and will be shipped and billed at the new actual price. The next priority will be the shipment of goods generated by new sales in the current quarter. If the total of all these operations entails a shortfall, that shortfall will be new back orders in the following quarter.

VALUE-ADDED TAX—Any VAT the firm collects for the government must be rebated each quarter. The VAT is a tax on the value you have added through the manufacturing process to the raw materials your company has purchased. In the simulation this is a tax on net revenue minus the value of all subassemblies found in the quarter's cost of goods sold. Tariffs are assessed at the country's rate on the actual price your firm received for the sets it sold.

NET SALES—An algebraic sum of all revenues associated with your company's main form of activity.

OTHER INCOME—Nonoperating revenue sources available to your company.

CAPITAL SALES GAINS/LOSSES—The net cash proceeds from plant and/or automated equipment sales to other companies in your industry.

INVESTMENT INCOME—Income earned on ninety-day short-term investments.

LICENSES—Income earned on patent licenses granted to other firms.

NONOPERATING INCOME—The algebraic sum of the three previous items. This constitutes income from activities incidental to your company's main manufacturing and sales activities.

TOTAL REVENUE—The sum of all previous items.

COST OF GOODS SOLD—The unit manufacturing costs of all products sold during the quarter. This is basically the unit costs for television sets you produced yourself or those obtained from other company-owned units through transfers in or contract manufacturing performed for you by other firms in the industry. For sales that have been through intracompany transfers, your unit cost is the transfer price used to make the transfer, which included shipping costs and administrative overhead. For intercompany transfers-in or manufacturing contract sales, your unit cost is the transfer price agreed upon by both parties, with the purchaser paying the shipping costs involved.

ADVERTISING—The unit's total advertising budget.

GENERAL ADMINISTRATION—The unit's total expenses for top executive compensation, a liaison executive to coordinate the activities of each country market in operation, factory superintendancy, line supervision and severance pay for any discharged supervisors, the plant's size based on the available labor hours, supervising new plant construction/expansion, equipment purchases and transfers and shut-down and continuing security costs on any decommissioned or liquidated factories.

SALES OFFICES—The quarter's total lease and administrative expenses for all sales offices in operation. This amount does not include the salaries and commissions earned by sales representatives attached to each sales office, but includes the salaries, hiring, firing, and moving expenses of any personnel associated with the firms sales office.

DISTRIBUTION CENTERS—All expenses associated with distribution center operations. This amount includes the costs of warranty work performed at each center, administrative overhead, and lease payments, but not unit inventory and handling charges. If an area does not have a distribution center and all goods are shipped directly from the market/country's factory, warranty work is both performed and charged at the plant level.

WHOLESALE OPERATIONS—The quarter's total expenses for all wholesale operations, regardless of whether they are C-wholesalers (company-owned wholesalers) or I-wholesalers (independent wholesalers). C-wholesaler expenses include any sales office start-ups, overhead, and shut-downs associated with sales offices tied to the C-wholesaler and its own its start-up and shut-down costs, leases, and staff salaries.

SALES FORCE SALARIES—Salaries and commissions to all sales representatives on the unit's payroll. Sales reps who quit the company leave on the quarter's last day and collect all monies owed them at that time.

TRAINEES—Salaries for all personnel in training in your firm's sales office(s).

TRAINING AND DEVELOPMENT—Your unit's training and development budget for the quarter. This account combines the individual budgets you have appropriated for training line workers, automation technicians, and sales representatives.

INVENTORY CHARGES—Inventory carrying and handling charges on the number of subassemblies and finished goods held in inventory on the previous operating quarter's last day. Inventory charges are not incurred on contract sales by your firm to other firms in your industry or for any sets you make for Home Electronics King.

SHIPPING—Shipping charges on products obtained for inventory through intercompany manufacturing contract sales, subassemblies received from your components consolidator in Hong Kong, and products shipped from your factories to your distribution centers. The shipping costs associated with the purchase of new automatons are considered part of the acquisition costs of adding or building new plant capacity, and are capitalized and subsequently depreciated. The same accounting procedures apply to the interfirm and intrafirm sale or transfer of used automatons. Contract and private-label sales are shipped FOB your factory, and these units do not go through your distribution centers.

LICENSE FEES—Payments made by your firm to other companies for the use of their patented products.

RESEARCH AND DEVELOPMENT—Your unit's research and development budget for the quarter.

QUALITY CONTROL—Your unit's quality control budget for the quarter.

DEPRECIATION—The quarter's total depreciation charges on fixed plant and equipment. A twenty-year depreciation schedule applies to plant and equipment, with a ten-year depreciation schedule earmarked for automatons. This is a noncash expense.

MAINTENANCE—Your unit's maintenance budget for the quarter. This amount is the total of individual budgets for general factory and assembly line maintenance, and maintenance by automaton type.

INTEREST CHARGES—This section gathers the interest charges on all the forms of debt your firm has used during the quarter.

OVERDRAFTS—Overdrafts associated with interest expenses forced on your company's corporate operations due to cash shortfalls in any of your operating units that cannot be covered by your home country unit's cash account. Because your corporate-level operations are ultimately responsible and accountable for the solvency of all market/country area operations, all cash shortfalls must be covered at your company's corporate level. Should country area operations place your corporation into technical bankruptcy, an overdraft is issued at the consolidated level.

SHORT-TERM LOAN—Interest expenses associated with an operating unit's ninety-day loan.

BONDS—The interest charge on the face value and nominal interest rate on all your company's outstanding bonds. Should the operating unit call all or a portion of its outstanding bond debt, the portion called will appear as an expense in this account, with the portion of the unamortized bond discount being called charged against current earnings.

MISCELLANEOUS—This includes three items: Merlin Group research studies; fines, penalties, or credits issued by the game administrator; and assorted costs associated with critical incident responses.

TOTAL EXPENSES—The sum of all expenses incurred during the quarter.

INCOME BEFORE TAXES—Total revenues less total expenses for the quarter.

INCOME BEFORE TAXES—Taxable income. If negative, a tax credit will be retained as an offset against future positive profits.

INCOME TAX—Federal and local taxes collected on all operating unit profits. Taxes are collected on a quarterly basis. If income is negative, the negative amount will be counted for tax credit purposes and offsets on positive earnings for three years or twelve quarters.

DIVIDEND TAX—Any taxes levied by foreign governments on retained earnings repatriated to the company's home country. These taxes have already been paid at the country/market level by the time they are consolidated at the headquarters level.

NET INCOME—Your operating unit's earnings after all taxes and expenses have been paid.

NORTH AMERICAN CONSOLIDATED BALANCE SHEET—A line identifying the market area's operations. Identical sheets are supplied for the APEC and EU market areas.

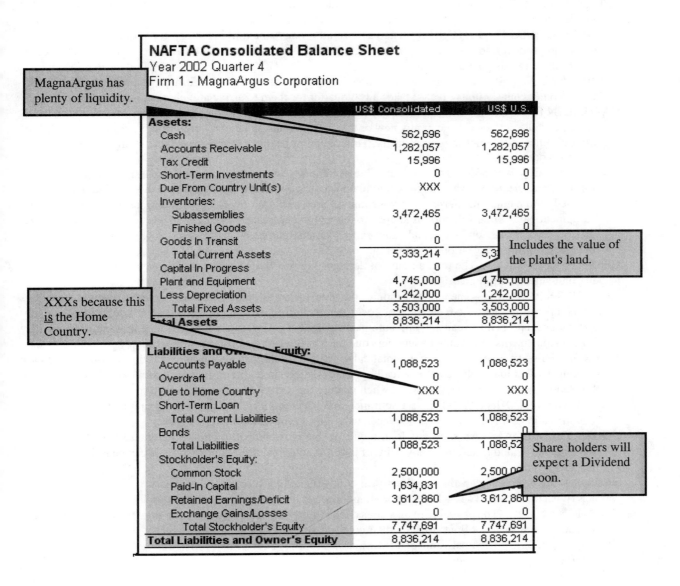

FIRM 1 MAGNAARGUS CORPORATION—A line identifying the company number as well as the unique name you have created for your company as part of the firm initialization process.

CASH—All cash assets held by the area operation and currently available for cash flow purposes during the next quarter.

ACCOUNTS RECEIVABLE—Monies owed your firm by your independent wholesale customers. This amount is collected and will be available to your firm the following quarter. Through a tight credit policy and mandatory performance bonds, all accounts are paid in full within ninety days of the following business quarter.

TAX CREDIT—A record of your firm's cumulative negative profits, which serve as tax credits.

SHORT-TERM INVESTMENTS—The total value of any investments your company has made in its respective local ninety-day money markets. This amount returns to the cash account on the first day of the next operating quarter, with the interest earned on the investments also going to the firm's cash account.

DUE FROM COUNTRY UNIT(S)—The value of all monies advanced to any country units in operation. The foreign country's credit rating will be very poor until these funds are repatriated to the home country.

SUBASSEMBLIES INVENTORIES—The market value of all grades and groups of subassemblies available for production in the next quarter based on their purchase price during the acquisition quarter.

FINISHED GOODS INVENTORIES—The value of all products held in inventory at the quarter's end after all sales and product transfers have been conducted. This figure is the weighted average of the unit costs of all contributors to this pool of products.

GOODS IN TRANSIT—The administered or transfer "price" value of all intrafirm goods being shipped by surface to other country units given it takes a full quarter for them to arrive at their destination.

CAPITAL IN PROGRESS—The value of any plant construction being conducted by the firm within the hemisphere and the net book value of any new or used automatons being purchased from your machine-tool supplier or other companies in your industry. This capital in progress begins to depreciate in the first quarter it becomes operational.

PLANT AND EQUIPMENT—The original value of all new plant and equipment, the purchase price of the land for the plant, the market value of used automatons purchased from other firms, and the remaining book value on used automatons transferred into your market area's operations. Once built and installed, the plant and equipment part of this valuation is subject to a twenty-year straight-line depreciation rate of 1/20th per year or 1/80th per quarter on its original value except for automatons, which depreciate on a ten-year schedule at the rate of 1/10th per year or 1/40th per quarter.

LESS DEPRECIATION—The total amount of depreciation that has occurred on all assets owned by the operating unit since their purchase date.

ACCOUNTS PAYABLE—The value of monies payable during the next operating quarter. Consists of portions of the operating quarter's factory labor costs, general administration expenses, advance purchases of subassemblies, and plant expansion and automaton purchases. The values reported here may not track exactly due to adjustments in payouts to suppliers due to cash flow exigencies and surpluses.

OVERDRAFT—An emergency loan automatically granted by the simulation to cover any total-company cash shortages. This loan will be automatically paid off by the simulation through its own cash flow operations, but should be taken into consideration when making the next quarter's cash projections.

DUE TO HOME COUNTRY—This is a nonfunctioning account for the home country unit but is active for any country unit, as it reflects monies advanced to it at the consolidated corporate level.

SHORT TERM LOAN—A ninety-day loan requested by your company. This loan's interest is charged in the current quarter and is automatically paid off in the simulation's following quarter. It can be rolled over quarter after quarter.

BONDS—The original face value of all ten-year bonds floated by your operating unit.

STOCKHOLDER'S EQUITY—The sum of all monies owed to the company's shareholders.

COMMON STOCK—The par value of all shares outstanding. This account is inoperative at the country unit level, as country units cannot float stock on their own account.

PAID-IN CAPITAL—The total value of all stock issues selling above or below par. This account is inoperative at the foreign country unit level.

RETAINED EARNINGS/DEFICIT—An account that accumulates all past and current quarter earnings and serves as the source for dividend declarations.

EXCHANGE GAINS/LOSSES—The algebraic sum of currency gains and losses obtained during the quarter.

MARKET/COUNTRY OPERATIONS REPORT

The next set of reports is unique to your company's operations. Depending on the number of market areas and products available to you, a number of market/country area reports are generated by the simulation. In these reports the data are usually reported in units of products, although at various times interest rate percentages, indexes, and ratings are displayed.

OPERATIONS REPORT—An indication of the type of report being presented.

YEAR 2002 QUARTER 4— The year and quarter of operations being reported.

FIRM 1 MAGNAARGUS CORPORATION—The firm being reported.

CREDIT RATING—The credit rating associated with each country operation. This rating is highly dependent on the firm's current liquidity, its total debt/equity ratio, and its times-interest-earned coverage. This rating ranges from AAA to C, with a AAA rating representing a firm entitled to the unit country's prime rate for short-term loans and the home country's federal government ten-year bond rate plus 1.0 percentage point. A C rating indicates a firm that has fallen into technical insolvency during the current quarter.

BOND RATE—The nominal or face rate applicable to ten-year bonds by each country operation. This rate is greatly influenced by the firm's liquidity, its debt management skills as indicated by its credit rating, and its amount of owners' equity given its total long-term debt. The effective rate, or the actual interest rate, charged for any bond issue is the result of the interaction between the firm's liquidity and equity value and the yield rates prevailing in the market/country area's major money market. In this case the money market area is New York City.

INTEREST RATE—The interest rate for a ninety-day loan in the firm's home country money market, given the unit's credit rating.

UNIT SALES—A breakdown of the actual units sold through all channels available.

25″ TV SALES—The number of 25-inch television sets sold in each country through both C-wholesalers and I-wholesalers.

27″ TV SALES—The number of 27-inch television sets sold in each country through your company's channels of C-wholesalers and I-wholesalers.

CONTRACT SALES—The number of contract units sold by your company by set size and country. These can be contracted units manufactured for other firms in your industry or private-label sales to Home Electronics King.

MARKET SHARE—Your company's proportion of total units sold by product and market/country area. This statistic does not include contract sales made in the home country.

BACKORDERS—The number of back-ordered units for delivery next quarter. The delivery of these units takes precedence over the delivery of newly generated sales, but is of lower priority than shipments to other country units or contract sales.

LOST SALES—The number of units of sales lost during the quarter. These lost sales are the result of your firm stocking-out and a number of your wholesalers refusing to accept your back order offer. In any given quarter your firm's total actual sales could have been the sum of its units sold, back orders, and lost sales.

PRODUCTION—The number of units your company's factory actually produced by product and shift. Two shifts are available, with overtime operations available as a 25 percent extension of each plant's second shift.

LINE SUPERVISORS—The number of supervisors or foremen assigned to each factory. These supervisors are distributed across the quarter's assembly lines and shifts.

WORKERS—The number of factory workers who actually appeared for work by shift and by products. The total number of workers who actually appear is a function of each country labor force's culturally biased inclinations or "work ethic" for the type of work and wages provided by your firm, their health, and the number of legal holidays in force.

HOURS DELIVERED—The number of worker labor hours actually delivered by shift and by products. This amount is circumscribed by the availability of raw materials for products scheduled for production, the amount of training and supervision workers have received in previous quarters, equipment maintenance budgets, and your work crew's "work ethic." It is on this amount of hours, given the prevailing wage rates in your market/country area, that your factory's wage bill is calculated.

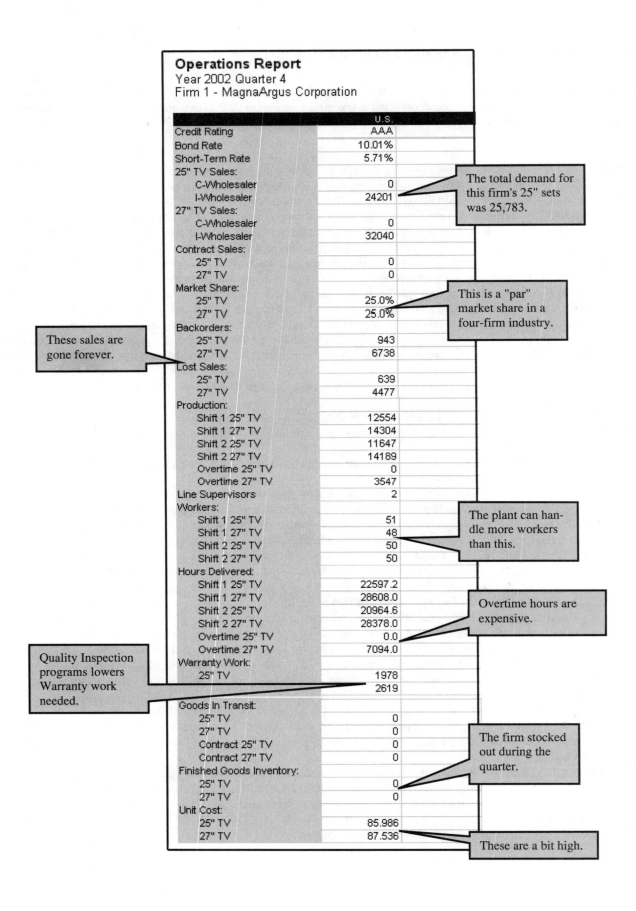

Operations Report
Year 2002 Quarter 4
Firm 1 - MagnaArgus Corporation

	U.S.
Credit Rating	AAA
Bond Rate	10.01%
Short-Term Rate	5.71%
25" TV Sales:	
C-Wholesaler	0
I-Wholesaler	24201
27" TV Sales:	
C-Wholesaler	0
I-Wholesaler	32040
Contract Sales:	
25" TV	0
27" TV	0
Market Share:	
25" TV	25.0%
27" TV	25.0%
Backorders:	
25" TV	943
27" TV	6738
Lost Sales:	
25" TV	639
27" TV	4477
Production:	
Shift 1 25" TV	12554
Shift 1 27" TV	14304
Shift 2 25" TV	11647
Shift 2 27" TV	14189
Overtime 25" TV	0
Overtime 27" TV	3547
Line Supervisors	2
Workers:	
Shift 1 25" TV	51
Shift 1 27" TV	48
Shift 2 25" TV	50
Shift 2 27" TV	50
Hours Delivered:	
Shift 1 25" TV	22597.2
Shift 1 27" TV	28608.0
Shift 2 25" TV	20964.6
Shift 2 27" TV	28378.0
Overtime 25" TV	0.0
Overtime 27" TV	7094.0
Warranty Work:	
25" TV	1978
	2619
Goods In Transit:	
25" TV	0
27" TV	0
Contract 25" TV	0
Contract 27" TV	0
Finished Goods Inventory:	
25" TV	0
27" TV	0
Unit Cost:	
25" TV	85.986
27" TV	87.536

Annotations:

The total demand for this firm's 25" sets was 25,783.

This is a "par" market share in a four-firm industry.

These sales are gone forever.

The plant can handle more workers than this.

Overtime hours are expensive.

Quality Inspection programs lowers Warranty work needed.

The firm stocked out during the quarter.

These are a bit high.

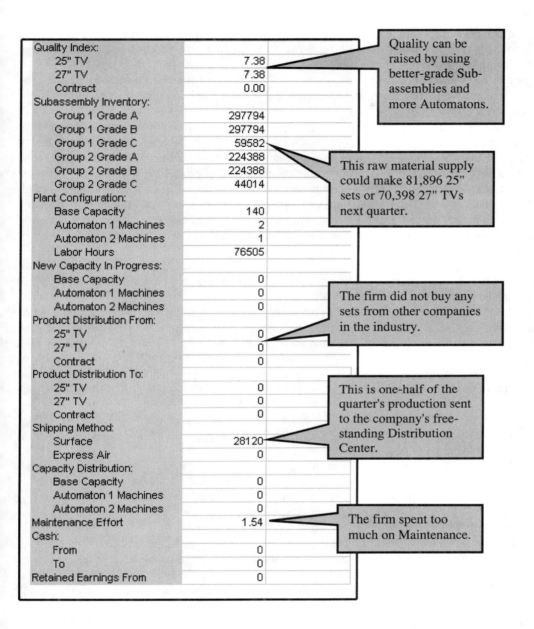

Quality Index:	
25" TV	7.38
27" TV	7.38
Contract	0.00
Subassembly Inventory:	
Group 1 Grade A	297794
Group 1 Grade B	297794
Group 1 Grade C	59582
Group 2 Grade A	224388
Group 2 Grade B	224388
Group 2 Grade C	44014
Plant Configuration:	
Base Capacity	140
Automaton 1 Machines	2
Automaton 2 Machines	1
Labor Hours	76505
New Capacity In Progress:	
Base Capacity	0
Automaton 1 Machines	0
Automaton 2 Machines	0
Product Distribution From:	
25" TV	0
27" TV	0
Contract	0
Product Distribution To:	
25" TV	0
27" TV	0
Contract	0
Shipping Method:	
Surface	28120
Express Air	0
Capacity Distribution:	
Base Capacity	0
Automaton 1 Machines	0
Automaton 2 Machines	0
Maintenance Effort	1.54
Cash:	
From	0
To	0
Retained Earnings From	0

Callouts: "Quality can be raised by using better-grade Sub-assemblies and more Automatons." "This raw material supply could make 81,896 25" sets or 70,398 27" TVs next quarter." "The firm did not buy any sets from other companies in the industry." "This is one-half of the quarter's production sent to the company's free-standing Distribution Center." "The firm spent too much on Maintenance."

WARRANTY WORK—The number of units upon which warranty work was performed by your firm's distribution centers and/or factories. The amount of warranty work required is a function of the quality control programs conducted during the quarter.

GOODS IN TRANSIT—The number of units in shipment by product to any non-home country operation via surface transportation. These goods take one quarter to arrive at their destination point. While in transit they remain on the sending unit's balance sheet. Upon their arrival the following quarter, the receiving unit's finished goods inventory is updated by the shipped-in amount. Its finished goods inventory account on its balance sheet will reflect the entire value of the shipment, whereas its cash account will be debited by this same value. The sending unit's cash account will be credited with the transfer price, and its finished goods inventory account will be debited by the same amount. Because private-label sales can only be made to a domestic retailer, shipments to them are not by air express. Contract sales, because they are negotiated far in advance, are shipped only by surface transportation and always appear as goods in transit for one quarter.

FINISHED GOODS INVENTORY—The total number of products held in temporary storage in your factories or distribution centers. All private-label TVs are shipped directly to the contracting retailer and therefore do not enter your firm's finished goods inventory.

UNIT COST—The average unit cost of your company's products and any private-label TVs you have made. The cost reported here is the weighted average of older units in inventory and those units possibly added in the current quarter.

QUALITY INDEX—An indication of the physical quality of the products produced in the operating quarter or sold via contract sales. Given the grades of subassemblies available to your company, the effective range of this index runs from 5.0 to 10.0, with a 5.0 indicating products of minimum quality, a 7.5 indicating an above average level of quality, and a 10.0 associated with the highest-quality products. For successful contract/private branding sales, the product's quality index must meet or exceed the quality grade contracted. For products made under license to other firms in your industry, you must produce your units at or above the quality index level specified in the contract. If this level is not attained during the contract's production quarter, the contract order is cancelled by the contracting firm and the sets are returned to your finished goods inventory for possible sale during the current quarter.

SUBASSEMBLY INVENTORY—The number of subassemblies available for next quarter's production by subassembly group and grade. Both groups of subassemblies are required to complete a television set, and these subassemblies can be purchased in three different quality grades.

PLANT CONFIGURATION—The mixture of assembly line-attended production methods, as possibly augmented by automatons of two levels of self-control and technical complexity. This mixture determines the engineering-based productivity of your firm's factories. The amount of production hours generated by the combination of workers and automatons is reported as total labor hours, which can be distributed among your products, given their assembly-labor-hour requirements. Base capacity is reported in the total number of workers that can staff each eight-hour shift. Automatons are reported in the number of Auto1s and Auto2s installed in each factory.

NEW CAPACITY IN PROGRESS—The incremental changes being made in your plant-operating capabilities through capacity expansions, new plant construction, or automaton acquisitions. The value reported here is shown for only the first quarter of capacity expansion or purchase.

PRODUCT DISTRIBUTION FROM/TO—A statement of the products actually shipped from and to various country units in the decision quarter. The number of units shipped may not equal the amounts you planned due to a number of factors, such as running out of raw materials, not scheduling enough line workers, or having equipment breakdowns. If a production shortfall occurs, your plant's logistics clerical will pro-rate the delivery of goods to the designated country units.

SHIPPING METHOD—A restatement of your firm's decisions on how to ship products within and between countries. Regular surface nondomestic shipments take one quarter for delivery and are reported as "goods in transit." All within-area shipments are delivered to distribution centers during the same quarter for sale. Express air (ExAir) shipping allows the receipt of all nondomestic products to other countries in the same quarter. Any combination of surface or express air shipping method applies to all shipments during the quarter.

CAPACITY DISTRIBUTION—A restatement of how your company distributed intercompany transfers of base capacity and automatons by automaton type and destination. These entries do not summarize those associated with any intrafirm asset sales to others in the industry, as these are separate buying/selling operations conducted outside your firm's usual line of business.

MAINTENANCE EFFORT—An index of the suitability of the operating unit's maintenance budget. Values above 1.00 indicate excessive maintenance funds; values below 1.00 indicate an inadequate amount of maintenance money was budgeted. If this condition is chronic, the plant's equipment begins to break down, labor hour productivity falls, and worker absentee rates increase.

CASH—A statement of how you transferred cash between companies.

RETAINED EARNINGS FROM—A statement of how you asked any offshore operations to remit their own retained earnings to your home country's retained earnings account. Because of dividend taxes levied in each foreign country, the amount of retained earnings ultimately arriving at headquarters will be less than the stated amount.

YOUR NEXT STEPS

You have now been presented with the basic types of outputs *The Global Business Game* produces. At this point many player want to "dive in" and start making decisions. It is recommended, however, that you sit back, take a deep breath, and organize your company and your activities so you will be as successful as possible. A number of experiential exercises are available to you at the game's dedicated Web site that can help you at this time. The following exercise can be found under "Player Resources" at the Web site: http://www.swcollege.com/management/gbg/gbg.html:

Personal-Goal and Group Norm Setting—Helps you and your teammates learn about each other's motivations and to set high performance norms for your management group.

Executive Evaluation—Creates a method by which you can rate the performance of your teammates at the game's midpoint and end point.

External Analysis—Helps your firm to understand the three types of environments within which you are conducting your business.

Internal Analysis—Creates an inventory of your firm's resources while determining which ones have long-term strategic value.

Strategic Intent and Mission—Provides a self-generated inventory of your company and team's assets and how you will use them to achieve your company's goals and mission.

Strategy Choice and Implementation—Has your company create its strategy based upon your management team's resources, capabilities, and core competencies.

Organization Structure/Descriptions—Results in a clear picture of your company's reporting relationships and the tasks each member will perform.

Your game administrator may assign some of them to you or you may wish to use them yourself.

Just as this chapter has dealt with the game's outputs, the next chapter will begin to deal with your inputs to the game. These entail the many decisions you will have to make if you are to run a successful company. Chapter 3 covers the simulation's marketing and marketing-logistics operations, and chapter 4 takes you through your company's factory operations. All this takes money, and that is covered in chapter 5, which details the game's financial and accounting operations. Chapter 6 will tell you how to install your manual's CD and how to enter and retrieve your quarterly results. A number of decision-making aids are also available to you both at the game's Web site and in this manual's appendixes in the form of cash flow forecasting forms, *pro forma* income statements, and balance sheets.

Chapter 3

Marketing and
Marketing Logistics

Your company's major revenue source comes from selling television sets delivered to wholesale customers through your distribution centers. These sets can be manufactured by yourself, or you can get them through contract sales from other firms in your industry. These television sets, regardless of how they are obtained, are then distributed through wholesaling operations that you either own or use in cooperation with independent wholesalers who sell related home-electronics items. Shipments to these wholesalers are recorded as "sales" from your company's distribution centers or factories. If you make any television sets for a retailer's private-label program, those units will be shipped FOB directly to the retailer's distribution center from the factory producing them. Your TV sets, along with those of your rivals, are then retailed, where they meet the challenges of the marketplace.

Exhibit 3.1 traces the simple movement of goods from factory to wholesalers to retailers. To be a successful marketer, however, you must thoroughly understand the details of the markets you have entered or may enter in the future, as well as how to handle the logistics of supplying your wholesalers and distribution centers with the products you want to sell. This chapter provides details regarding the markets and market segments in which you can compete, the logistics of national and international product distribution, how preferential demand for your television sets can be accomplished, and how you can obtain proprietary information about your markets and marketing efforts.

DEMAND CREATION

The factors affecting the general demand for television sets and the seasonal demand factor associated with each country market has already been presented in Chapter 1. Although your firm has little influence on each marketing area's macroeconomic and socioeconomic factors, it *can* influence the derived demand for its branded television sets in a number of ways. This can be done through (1) changes and improvements in product quality and features; (2) the relative size of your quarterly advertising budgets; (3) the amount of service you provide your wholesalers through the number of distribution centers and sales offices you have; (4) the total number of wholesalers handling your products; and (5) the number of sales representatives you have and the types of sales-incentive programs you use to motivate them.

Product quality and product features pertain to the physical properties of your products. These physical changes are obtained through (1) research and development expenditures, which may result in obtaining a patented improvement in your products; (2) the quality of the subassemblies you use in each television set you make; (3) the level of quality control you obtain through your company's quality control budgets; and (4) the reliabilities of the two types of automatons your company uses in its manufacturing process. While these efforts physically differentiate your products, they can also be differentiated in a psychological sense. This is done through the prices you charge for your TVs, the strength of your sales promotions, and the distribution channel support you apply.

Sales promotion efforts entail the relative size of the advertising programs you conduct in your various geographic markets for each product sold by TV set size, the magnitude of your sales force(s), and your sales force's quality and enthusiasm. Sales force quality is determined by the amount of money you spend on its training and development, and enthusiasm or zeal is largely determined by the amount of incentives you use to encourage the staff to pursue sales.

The effectiveness of your advertising program is determined by factors both within and outside your company's control. The controllable factor is the size of your advertising budget on a product-by-product basis. The factors you cannot control are the sizes of your competitors' advertising budgets and each nation's ability to read and respond to your print advertisements. This latter factor is indicated by each country's literacy and newspaper readership rates, presented in the national profiles in Chapter 1.

Exhibit 3.1   Marketing Channels and Channel Participants

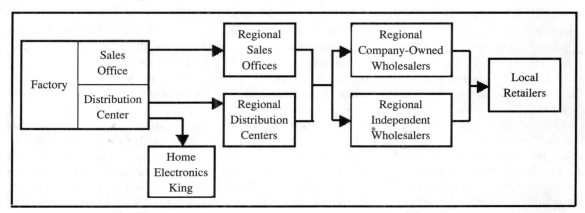

Channel support boosts your advertising programs, which tend to pull your products through the distribution channel, and the amount of service and delivery promptness you provide through the number of distribution centers you operate. The number of sales representatives you employ out of sales offices in each geographic market tends to push your products through each country's distribution channel. When adding new sales offices to those already in operation, your simulation will open the new office in the country's next largest city market. If you add more offices later, the simulation moves to the next largest city market. Accordingly, in the United States, your first sales office would be in New York City, the next office would be in Los Angeles, and the next would be in Chicago.

You can also control marketing channel operations by owning and conducting your own wholesale operations. If you do this, your firm must bear the risks and costs of the building and equipment leases associated with these company-owned wholesalers. On the other hand, you gain the dedicated efforts of this part of your wholesaling function.

PRODUCT PRICES AND BACK ORDERS

Many of your company's sales promotion activities are attempts to lessen the impact of raw prices on the demand for your products. To some degree you can do this, but product prices are still very important to your ultimate consumers. This is because your independent wholesalers want to stock the sets that are the easiest to sell, and low prices are very attractive to end-users. More important, manufacturer prices are multiplied as they go through the industry's distribution channels. Given the standard markups each channel participant expects to take, a relatively small change in the manufacturer's price is greatly magnified by the time it gets to the retail level.

It has become standard practice to use catalogue or "list prices" in your industry. While these are each firm's official prices, they are subject to the market's supply and demand pressures. Thus they are never the actual prices charged for the sets being sold. All list prices are subject to trade discounts, volume incentives, and unit-based slotting allowances you negotiate with your wholesalers. The total value of these trade incentives is reflected in the difference between each firm's list prices and each product's actual price. The global industry report lists each firm's list prices for the quarter. Actual prices are also reported, but this information has taken one quarter to collect and report accurately. Thus the "actual price" listed in the global industry report is for the previous quarter's prices by company.

Each firm's sales representatives are paid their commissions on list prices rather than actual prices. This is because each product's final price is not under the direct control of your sales reps, although you are encouraging them to conclude all sales as close to your list price as possible.

If your Sales reps write orders for more units than can be supplied by your firm that quarter, a back order condition will occur. This filling of the back orders receives a priority treatment in the following quarter, with these back orders taking a higher delivery priority than that given to the quarter's new orders. If your firm lowers a product's actual price between quarters, any back orders are filled at the lower price. The commission paid on these sales, still, will be on the list price that initially created the sale.

PRODUCT SEGMENTS

Within each country/market area, depending on the game's complexity, you may sell both models of your television sets except within your home country, where you can also dedicate some of your factory's capacity to manufacture sets for private or store-brand sales. Each of your nationally branded sets can be targeted for the industry's various price and quality segments through (1) the quality control measures taken by your company, (2) the degree of reliability fostered by the amount of automaticity you employed in your manufacturing processes, and (3) the quality mix of the subassembly grades found in each television set. For private-brand sales, announcements of bid requests by Home Electronics King will appear quarterly on the simulation's bulletin board. To win the bid for the quarter, your firm must be the lowest bidder while producing at or above the product quality grade index announced in the retailer's request.

Regarding your company's branded products, it appears to your customers that the industry's best sets are made from the finest materials available. The product's finish has a custom-made appearance, and the product experiences very few failures or warranty repairs and therefore is considered very reliable. In the simulation products in this league, use the highest-grade subassemblies and use highly automated and closely supervised manufacturing processes. Products in this category have consistently earned "best quality" ratings or quality indexes in the 8.70 to 10.00 range in various consumer magazines, such as *Consumer Reports*.

Of minimum quality are television sets with quality indexes ranging from 4.00 to 5.50. These products are very reliable but have fewer features that could malfunction, use good subassemblies that are less sophisticated, and employ a finished appearance that is pleasing but not highly crafted. The lowest-grade products have quality indexes below 4.00. These sets have often earned "best value" ratings in various consumers' digests and electronics magazines, although some break down under long-term use. In the United States, these would be products for mass market or discount stores. Other retailers often use these products as promotional items or as promotional traffic builders. These sets have relatively few convenience features and shorter life expectancies.

Your firm's retailers have traditionally given you much support. This is because your products have had generally high quality levels. Those companies in your industry that manufacture sets of lower quality have had difficulty getting retailers to stock their products once their customers started complaining about them. Exhibit 3.2 summarizes the characteristics of the product grades found for the television sets you can manufacture and/or sell.

When selling your sets in the different countries found in *The Global Business Game,* you will find that, as in the real world, each country is in a different life-cycle stage of its acceptance of these products. Thus these products are used for somewhat different purposes in each nation. You can capitalize on these usage differences by differentiating the quality, features, and prices of your offerings from country to country. For example, in the United States the proportion of customers buying new, basic-feature 25-inch sets may be comparatively low. In Thailand, such a set may be

Exhibit 3.2   Product Grades and Market Segments

Quality Index	Market Segment	Product Characteristics and Retailer Service
8.70–10.00	Select, high-price segment	Highest-grade materials; Custom-crafted appearance; Very reliable under heavy use; Electronics salon retailer service and "cutting edge" product features and conveniences; High retailer support.
6.01–8.69	Moderate-price segment; department store quality	Good-grade materials; Pleasing appearance; Very reliable under moderate use; Many convenience features.
1.00–6.00	Low-price segment; promotional and discount store quality	Basic-grade materials; Plain appearance; Base features; Minimal retailer selling and service support.

Exhibit 3.3 Distribution Center and Sales Office Start-Up and Shut-Down Costs (in local currencies)

Country	Distribution Centers		Sales Offices	
	Start-Up	Shut-Down	Start-Up	Shut-Down
United States	45,000	56,000	20,000	15,000
Mexico	297,000	360,000	14,200	10,600
Germany	77,700	96,700	34,500	25,900
Spain	34,700	43,100	15,400	11,500
Japan	5,200,000	7,740,000	2,150,000	4,410,000
Thailand	1,300,000	1,610,000	64,800	48,600

considered very desirable. For the more full-featured 27-inch sets, the demand may be higher in Germany than in the United States, due to the former country's greater interest in highly technical products. Alternatively, the typical German home is smaller, so a very reliable 25-inch set might be more desirable than a larger, less reliable 27-inch set.

Although it may be a good idea to target your offerings to certain market segments, the frequent switching from segment to segment on your company's part can lead to customer confusion. Some firms have found it best to stay in a particular price/feature/quality segment for several periods before attempting to upgrade or downgrade their television sets to match a segment's particular needs.

DISTRIBUTION CENTERS AND SALES OFFICES

In distributing your products, each factory initially operates as its own warehouse and sales office. Accordingly, if your company has a factory in a particular country, your firm automatically possesses one distribution center and one sales office. Should you wish to distribute products in a country where you do not have a factory, or you wish to have better coverage of a particular country market, your firm can lease warehousing space and sales offices according to the schedule in Exhibit 3.3.

If your firm wants to improve the service level it provides its wholesalers, and therefore obtain long-term goodwill and customer reorders, additional sales offices, which may or may not be attached to any company-owned wholesalers you may have, can be leased to accomplish these ends. Over the simulation's duration you can increase or decrease the number of sales offices operated within each country, as well as the number of distribution centers. The lease-cancellation penalty is the same regardless of the remaining number of quarters left on the lease being cancelled.

When choosing the number of sales offices you operate, as well as the number of sales representatives you want to assign to them, it would be wise to consider the geographic expanses and population densities involved in the countries within which you conduct business. You can assume that diminishing marginal returns on additional sales offices, distribution centers, and sales representatives will begin immediately after the leasing of your first additional sales office, distribution center, sales representative, or company-owned wholesaler. This is because your company has chosen a marketing policy of initially establishing itself in each country's most populous city and then moving sequentially to the next largest population area.

With more distribution centers, your firm obtains faster delivery times to its wholesalers within its particular geographic area as well as minimizing the shipping charges retailers must pay when getting your television sets from your distribution centers. This higher level of accessibility improves the service level you provide your wholesalers. And you can expect wholesalers to be more loyal to those companies that provide them with better service.

When determining the shipping charges your firm encounters during the business quarter to get your television sets to distribution centers, remember that your factory counts as one distribution center. Thus this factory-related distribution center does not require a shipping charge, as it simply ships products held temporarily in storage as they come off the assembly line. Shipping charges are incurred for getting goods to all your other domestic centers. These charges are spread equally over the number of distribution centers you have in operation, minus one for the factory's distribution operation. The following example demonstrates an activity that results in a $691,666 shipping charge appearing on an American-based country operation's income statement.

> 415,000 units shipped within the United States
> 5 distribution centers
> 1 factory distribution operation
> 69,167 units shipped per distribution operation (415,000/6)
> 345,833 units shipped to distribution centers
> 69,167 units distributed by factory distribution operation
> US$691,666 shipping charges incurred (345,833 × $2.00)

SHIPPING METHODS

Under normal conditions you will probably be making your shipments by regular surface transportation to your distribution centers. This is an inexpensive and relatively reliable method for domestic operations. For overseas sales, however, it is very slow. For operations between the United States and Germany, for instance, between loading your TVs on rail cars in Erie, Pennsylvania, and delivering them to the port in Newark, New Jersey, then shipping them across the Atlantic Ocean to the German port of Hamburg for rail shipping within Germany itself, a number of months will have elapsed. Because all sales, except those that are made either under contract or for private-label purposes, are made through your firm's distribution centers, all orders must be filled from these centers. Accordingly, they must be fully stocked at the beginning of the quarter, or experience enough inboard shipments during the quarter to allow them to make all their sales, thereby avoiding back orders and causing possible customer dissatisfaction. You can assume, unless express air shipping methods are employed, that all shipments within a country can be completed during the quarter and that shipments between countries or continents take one quarter to complete.

Through careful planning, you can save your firm money by using only regular surface shipping. There may be occasions, however, when you have misplanned, have experienced greater sales during the previous quarter than anticipated, or merely would like to speed up your firm's inventory cycle. If this is the case, you can service any of your distribution centers by using express air (ExAir) shipments.

As shown in Exhibit 3.4, the ExAir rate is about three times higher than the surface rate. Your firm, however, may feel this higher cost is compensated for because you will not have dissatisfied retailers seeking other wholesale suppliers in future quarters. When making your quarter's decision, you must indicate the total number of units that are

Exhibit 3.4   Unit Shipping Rates (in dollars)

Geographic Market	Shipping Method	
	Surface	ExAir
Within North America	2.00	6.20
North America to Europe	9.00	27.90
North America to Asia	12.00	36.00
Within Europe	2.50	7.48
Europe to North America	10.00	30.50
Europe to Asia	15.50	48.70
Within Asia	4.50	13.50
Asia to North America	8.50	52.75
Asia to Europe	18.00	53.80

to be shipped to each country by set size. If both shipping methods are used during the quarter, all sets will be shipped proportionally to the total number of sets being shipped surface and air express. As an example the following product distribution would result in 2,500 25-inch TVs surface-shipped to Mexico and 1,500 air-expressed to the same country. Spain would receive 938 25-inch sets via surface and 562 by air express. Respective 27-inch sets' surface and ExAir shipments to Mexico would be 1,250 and 750 units, while Japan's would be 312 and 188 units.

Product Distribution	Units
25″ TV Distribution to Mexico	4,000
25″ TV Distribution to Spain	1,500
27″ TV Distribution to Mexico	2,000
27″ TV Distribution to Japan	500
Surface Shipping	5,000
Express Air Shipping	3,000

INVENTORY HANDLING CHARGES

Your company's products are very durable so they are not subject to deterioration under normal warehousing conditions. Because of this, the direct inventory charges for your finished goods are fairly low on a per unit basis. Handling charges, however, are somewhat high for your company's television sets because of their fragile components. The handling charges for your 27-inch set are slightly higher than for your 25-inch sets, as your larger sets are more complex and have more parts that can be broken. No handling and inventory charges are due on contract or private-label sets, as these are shipped directly to the recipient's own facilities.

The inventory and product handling costs involved are presented in Exhibit 3.5. They will appear as part of the inventory charges on your company's income statement and are incurred on all units produced during the quarter, because all units are ultimately handled and inventoried at some level within your firm's physical distribution system.

Exhibit 3.5   Inventory and Handling Charges by Product (in local currencies)

Country		Product	
		25-Inch	27-Inch
United States:	Inventory	.75	.80
	Handling	1.20	1.30
Mexico:	Inventory	.50	.56
	Handling	.85	.90
Germany:	Inventory	1.40	1.54
	Handling	2.49	2.53
Spain:	Inventory	.63	.68
	Handling	1.03	1.11
Japan:	Inventory	96.50	101.50
	Handling	155.00	160.00
Thailand:	Inventory	2.40	2.60
	Handling	3.83	4.15

Exhibit 3.6	Quarterly Distribution Center and Sales Office Overhead Costs (in local currencies)	

	Operation	
Country	Distribution Centers	Sales Offices
United States	110,000	86,000
Mexico	78,000	60,300
Germany	190,100	148,600
Spain	84,800	66,300
Japan	13,600,000	10,940,000
Thailand	342,200	278,000

Exhibit 3.7	Independent Wholesaler Servicing Costs (in local currencies)
Country	Cost
United States	11,000
Mexico	27,200
Germany	19,000
Spain	8,485
Japan	1,350,000
Thailand	24,600

DISTRIBUTION CENTER AND SALES OFFICE EXPENSES

The administrative charges and general overhead and operational expenses associated with each distribution center and sales office represent fairly fixed costs regardless whether the centers operate out of your factories or are leased. Because of this fixed-cost nature, there are certain economies of scale that can be realized in your company's logistics function. Exhibit 3.6 itemizes the charges linked to each country and its operation. These charges include lease payments, heat, light and utilities, and front-office salaries.

INDEPENDENT WHOLESALE OPERATIONS

Your company, as is the industry's norm, has used independent wholesalers in the past to service its customers. These wholesalers handle a large number of products from other manufacturers, but none of these products competes directly with yours. In this regard each wholesaler is totally dedicated to taking orders for your television sets from its retail customers, as well as engaging in a modest amount of its own wholesale advertising.

Because they are independent wholesalers with years of experience in the electronic appliance business, they require minimal attention from your company's sales representatives. Thus the cost of servicing or supporting each independent wholesaler is rather low, as shown by country in Exhibit 3.7. An additional benefit in using independent wholesalers lies in the fact that they lighten the load on your sales representatives and allow them to work more directly with retailers to promote the sale of your products.

COMPANY-OWNED WHOLESALE OPERATIONS

In your industry the use of independent wholesalers has been the standard practice for many years. However, each independent wholesaler sells a wide range of products and their attentions are naturally divided. Also, their natural loyalties are to themselves rather than to *your* company. This situation has begun to change. With the arrival of super stores and category killer and big box retail operations, the bargaining power between retailers and their wholesalers has shifted. With small, local wholesaling operations under threat, a number of home-electronics manufacturers have begun to create their own wholesale operations as well as attempting to countervail the bargaining power of these larger retailers.

When you create your own wholesalers, you obtain their full-time dedication to your products while retaining for them the standard 40.0 percent markup on merchandise cost the independent wholesalers have needed in the past to cover their own expenses.

Exhibit 3.8   Company-Owned Wholesaling Operations Costs (in local currencies)

Country	Start-Up	Shut-Down	Quarterly Lease	Salaries
United States	35,000	52,500	3,000	60,000
Mexico	24,700	37,000	24,400	42,500
Germany	60,600	91,200	40,900	103,000
Spain	26,700	40,200	18,100	45,500
Japan	4,500,000	6,900,000	390,000	7,500,000
Thailand	114,000	171,000	117,000	194,600

By creating your own wholesalers, however, your company has to bear the fixed-cost risks associated with leasing arrangements and certain semi-variable personnel costs. Independent wholesalers are almost free, as they require minimal attention by your company—although you must provide them with the markups they need so they can make a reasonable profit.

Should you wish to create a number of your own wholesaling operations, with each one possessing its own sales office, your company would be subject to the schedule presented in Exhibit 3.8. This covers the quarterly salaries of personnel associated with each operation, the initial start-up costs, overhead and lease costs, and any shut-down costs should you want to cease a wholesaling operation and eliminate its quarterly salaries. The salaries presented in this exhibit do not include those of the sales representatives assigned to the market territory.

The amount of business each company-owned wholesaler does is based on the mix of independent and company-owned wholesalers your firm uses. It is assumed you would place your own wholesalers in each country market's most important local markets, using independent wholesalers to fill out your country's coverage.

On this basis your first company-owned wholesaler would contribute the most to your country's sales volume, with each succeeding company-owned wholesaler contributing less and less to total sales. When deciding on the optimum mix between independent and company-owned wholesale operations, remember that your company's total sales is partially determined by the total number of wholesalers you have selling your products.

When calculating the margins your company receives on television sets sold by your own wholesalers, you can assume that your revenue on each sale would be your manufacturer's actual price plus the standard 40.0 percent wholesaler's markup on cost. As an example, assume that the actual price to independent wholesalers of your 25-inch sets is $105 per unit. That wholesaler would mark the sets up to $147.00 for sale to retailers. If those sets were sold to the same retailers by your company-owned wholesaler, the independent wholesaler's markup would be your own. In this case, this amounts to $42 a unit. This markup recovery, however, is not free. You must now bear the costs of running a wholesale operation, which means you would be spending much more to get an equal amount of geographic coverage of your country's market.

INTRACOMPANY TRANSFERS

Your company can produce products in one area and sell them in another. You can also ship finished goods between countries for distribution from your regional distribution centers. In the past, your firm has set its intracompany transfer price by marking up its unit production costs by 10.0 percent. The simulation will maintain this policy by adding a factor of 1.10 to any sending unit's direct manufacturing costs on a per set basis. This markup covers the producing factory's overhead expenses, with the receiving country/market absorbing the product's transportation costs.

When making intracompany shipments, the sending country's factory ships the products to distribution centers in the designated country market before it makes product shipments to its own domestic distribution center(s). Therefore, foreign transfers have a priority over shipments to domestic distribution center(s) and the filling of any back orders obtained in the previous quarter. When shipments are made, the sending factory's inventory valuation is decreased by the standard transfer price, and its cash account is increased by the same amount. The receiving country's inventory valuation is increased by this same transfer price, and its cash account is decreased by this valuation plus the associated shipping charges that are borne by the receiving country unit. These shipping charges will also appear on the receiving country's income statement for the quarter.

All monetary transactions are done at the exchange rates existing between countries during the quarter the transfers occur—except for transfers of products between Spain and Germany, whose rates are fixed under the new, euro-based monetary system. When making shipments to a country's distribution center either from your company's factories or to other distribution centers, you can assume that your products will be optimally disbursed among all centers operating within each country.

SALES FORCE SIZE

As your firm enters new sales territories, or as you experience personnel turnovers, you will have to take steps to maintain or increase the number of sales representatives you have in the field. You can do this through two methods. One method is to train new people for sales openings that may eventually occur. The second method is to hire experienced sales representatives away from other firms.

It is important that you maintain a steady, experienced, and well-trained sales force. The best method you have for doing this is to pay it competitive salaries. When you do, Sales reps do not seek employment with other firms. Despite any outstanding salaries you may pay, however, it is quite likely you will always experience Sales rep "quits." This is because they want to move to other cities, go to other companies just for a change of scenery, or their spouses made career moves. Your objective, then, is to guard against a higher number of quits than is normal for firms with sales staffs of your size.

If your company wants to increase its sales force, the least expensive way is to plan ahead and train new hires in your sales offices. When they are in training, your trainees are paid the salaries that apply to them in Exhibit 3.9 by county. All trainees must be held in their training programs for at least one quarter. Thereafter they can be moved into the field at the costs shown in the same exhibit. Once in the field they earn the same base salaries and are subject to the same commission schedules that apply to the rest of your sales staff.

Training new people in advance of your current needs is a relatively low-cost option. You may wish, however, to move more quickly. This is done by hiring experienced sales representatives. If you do this, your company uses the services of an outside personnel search firm. You pay its recruiting fee, as well as the moving expenses incurred by each newly hired sales rep, in the quarter she or he joins your company.

Given the market's fluctuations, it is entirely possible you may place too many people in the field, or have put too many in training. To make a downward adjustment in your sales staff, you can dismiss or fire them from their positions. There are no costs attached to firing trainees, as they have not yet attained a "career" status in your company. The firing of veteran sales representatives is another matter. Out of appreciation for their past efforts, your firm's policy has been to provide each dismissed sales rep with a severance package that combines money with outplacement services. The costs associated with the implementation of this policy in each country are also presented in Exhibit 3.9.

Exhibit 3.9   Sales Force Hiring, Firing, and Deployment Costs (in local currencies)

Country	Sales Representatives			Trainees	
	Hiring	Firing	Moving	Salary	Moving
United States	11,000	6,000	8,680	9,100	3,000
Mexico	4,680	1,100	1,800	5,850	1,200
Germany	15,800	5,200	19,100	18,400	8,000
Spain	7,000	2,300	8,400	4,500	3,400
Japan	1,400,000	840,000	1,050,000	850,000	300,000
Thailand	120,202	71,300	15,300	72,300	10,200

When you submit your sales force decisions each quarter, the simulation will comply with any requests you make. Thus if your sales force initially had ten sales reps in the United States and your entry for the decision quarter was eight sales reps, the simulation would assume you wanted to fire two sales representatives. This action would be taken and a charge of $12,000 would be added to your sales force expenses for the quarter. The dismissal of trainees operates in the same fashion. If you were training three sales reps in the previous quarter and your entry for this quarter was one trainee with none being moved into the field, the simulation would remove two trainees from your company's sales office training program.

The simulation will also operate in an intelligent fashion regarding the use of the sales personnel available. Because of language barriers, however, sales reps cannot be moved between countries. As an example of how the simulation handles the deployment of sales representatives, if your past quarter's sales reps totaled eleven in Germany, and you wanted to have three representatives added to the German sales force while already having two trainees in your sales offices, the simulation would automatically move the two trainees into the field while hiring one experienced sales rep off the street. The associated charges of 50,280 euros would be added to your country unit's sales force expense for the decision quarter.

SALES REPRESENTATIVES AND SALES-INCENTIVE PROGRAMS

The quality of your company's selling force is important at the local sales office level. This quality level is related to the size of your company's training and development budget within each country and the number of sales representatives you have. Within each country, a minimal base salary appears to be appropriate given local wage and salary rates. To this base salary your company may want to apply a per unit commission on each of your company's branded sets. On your firm's decision form, this per unit commission is stated as a percent of the firm's list price for each size of television set you are selling. No commissions are paid on contract sales, as they are negotiated by a separate office in your home country's headquarters.

Your sales force's quality is also a function of its turnover rate. As your sales force's turnover increases, its overall effectiveness is diminished. This is because customer relationships are broken and new sales representatives must establish their credentials with wholesalers. As the simulation progresses you will be informed of the loss of sales representatives through messages found in your company report. Experienced sales representatives are immediately paid the base salary you have established in the countries in which they were hired and assigned.

IMPORT TARIFFS, TRADING COMMUNITIES, AND TRADING ZONES *NAFT*

Various countries, either by themselves or jointly through such trading communities as NAFTA, EU, or APEC, have used tariff policies over the years. These policies are intended to stimulate trade within particular areas, provide revenues for the governments affected, and/or protect domestic manufacturers and their workers' jobs from foreign competition. Through tariff actions a country makes foreign products more expensive for domestic consumption, thereby making the domestically produced product comparatively less expensive—regardless of its intrinsic quality or value. Tariff actions, however, often cause foreign governments to impose retaliatory tariffs.

Some of these aspects of tariff policy can be seen in the rate schedules shown in Exhibits 3.10 and 3.11 (page 34). The first of these two exhibits displays the tariff rates set by each trading zone. For the purposes of this business game, it is assumed that NAFTA, EU, and APEC are in full effect, but in a simplified fashion. Within-zone tariffs are very low or nonexistent, but fairly restrictive tariffs have been applied to all products entering from countries outside each trading zone. These trading zone tariffs are added to each country's own tariff, if one exists. Exhibit 3.11 shows the tariff rates each country has established for itself against the television sets made in other countries both inside and outside their own trading zones.

As an example of how tariffs operate, if an American firm wanted to sell its television sets to customers in Japan, it would have to pay a 7.0 percent trading zone tariff and a 1.6 percent country tariff, for a total tariff charge of 8.6 percent on the product's actual selling price, but *not* its list price. As a general rule, the United States has been relatively

Exhibit 3.10   Trading Zone Tariff Rates

	Receiving Zone		
Sending Zone	**NAFTA**	**EU**	**APEC**
NAFTA	0.0%	4.0%	7.0%
EU	3.0%	0.0%	7.0%
APEC	3.0%	5.0%	0.0%

Exhibit 3.11   Country Tariff Rates

	Receiving Country					
Sending Country	**United States**	**Mexico**	**Germany**	**Spain**	**Japan**	**Thailand**
United States	0.0%	0.0%	1.6%	1.6%	1.6%	1.6%
Mexico	0.0%	0.0%	0.0%	5.3%	0.0%	0.0%
Germany	4.7%	2.0%	0.0%	0.0%	1.0%	4.6%
Spain	1.7%	4.0%	0.0%	0.0%	8.0%	1.0%
Japan	0.5%	1.0%	3.0%	7.0%	0.0%	0.3%
Thailand	6.0%	0.0%	4.6%	3.0%	0.3%	0.0%

open to foreign competition, whereas many Asian countries have been relatively closed to outside competition. The tariff rates in these exhibits will be in effect at the beginning of your simulation, but changes in the world's political and economic situation during the simulation may cause various countries to alter their tariff policies.

Should your firm engage in any intrafirm product transfers, the tariffs shown in Exhibits 3.10 and 3.11 will be assessed on the transfer price that was established and will be charged to the receiving country unit. It is assumed that the country's tariff charge is passed on to consumers through the nation's distribution channels, thereby putting foreign-made products at a competitive price disadvantage. The tariffs your firm collects must be rebated each quarter to the country unit's federal government, as you are merely acting as its tax collector. In the simulation these tariffs will automatically be deducted from the country unit's cash flow operation for the quarter.

RESEARCH AND DEVELOPMENT

Although the television industry is in its mature stage, new developments are always occurring in electronics technology. Thus it would be a good idea to engage in a steady program of research. As your firm engages in these efforts, it might even make a discovery that results in an improvement or a modest innovation that is patentable and has commercial value. This patent, when applied to your television sets, either enhances the set's picture quality or its sound system, or provides a new, highly desirable convenience feature. Thus your firm will obtain a modest competitive advantage, which applies automatically to all TV sets you produce. The strength of this advantage will be greatest during the first quarter of its use, although residual strength will last for almost a year. After about one year, your innovation will be effectively duplicated by others in your industry.

When your R&D monies have produced a patentable innovation, you will receive confidential written notification of this fact as part of your firm's operations report. Products improved by this innovation will go on sale in the following quarter. Any existing goods in the current quarter's finished goods inventory will be retrofitted with the patented feature as part of your company's existing R&D budget.

Getting a patented product improvement requires a number of quarters of R&D projects. Your company should first determine an R&D budget policy and then engage in a steady implementation of that policy. Only through steady budgets will your firm obtain a patentable feature. There is no limit to the number of patents your firm can receive, as any number of research projects can be in operation simultaneously within your firm.

PATENTS AND CROSS-LICENSING AGREEMENTS   ok

Your firm can also purchase from another firm one of its patented features and can offer your most recent patented feature to other companies in your industry. To accomplish either of these actions, you must notify the game administrator that you have a patented feature you would like to buy or sell and at what price. Your game administrator will cause the simulation to place an announcement of your offer on the global industry report's bulletin board.

To complete the purchase or sale of a patented feature, both parties must use the "Patent Licensing Sale and Patent Transfer Agreement" form found in Appendix F of your Player's Manual. This form must be used for each patent-licensing sale or transfer. It must be (1) properly signed and approved by the game administrator; (2) signed by both parties to the transaction; and (3) submitted with your decision set for the quarter in which the transaction is to occur. The competitive advantage time frame cited for the firm that created the patented innovation will immediately accrue to the firm obtaining the patent for its own use.

INTERCOMPANY CONTRACTS AND JOINT-LICENSING VENTURES   ok

In addition to being able to transfer your company's patents or buy patents from others, you can engage in joint-licensing ventures. In conducting these ventures, one firm contracts to provide another firm an agreed-upon number of units of product at a negotiated price and quality level. The contracted units are automatically shipped to the purchaser's distribution center at the shipping rate applicable to the geographic area within which the units were fabricated with the shipping costs paid by the purchasing firm.

The sets contracted for will be shipped by surface and only if the product quality level specified in the contract is matched or exceeded by the contractee. Acceptable contracted units take priority over shipments and sales the selling company could obtain from its own distribution center. If the contracted TVs do not meet the quality level specified in the contract, they will not be shipped; instead they become part of the contractee's finished goods inventory for sale the next period.

The process by which your firm obtains such a joint-venture partner is initiated by submitting the "Product Sale and Transfer Agreement" form found in Appendix H of your Player's Manual. When you submit this form to your game administrator, your company will be listed on the industry report's bids and offers posting the following quarter. Should you obtain a potential joint-venture partner, the product, quality grade, and contract length of that venture should be certified and accepted by the game administrator and both joint-venture parties. After receiving the properly signed instruments, your game administrator will cause the contract to be implemented for the quarter specified in the joint-venture contract bid the selling firm should dedicate the required number of units under "Contracted Units" on GBG-Player's Logistics page.

MARKET RESEARCH

Your firm can elect to conduct market research as an aid to better understanding how your industry's markets operate. Although you would probably never be able to answer every question you might have about the markets in this game before making future decisions, a modest amount of market research can be conducted for you by the Merlin Group, Ltd. This group is a fairly new market research firm headquartered in San Jose, California. The types of research studies

Exhibit 3.12   Merlin Group, Ltd., Research and Rate Schedule (in dollars)

Question	Charge	Information Provided
1	1,500	All company 25″ TV unit sales by Country.
2	1,500	All company 27″ TV unit sales by Country.
3	500	Near-term forecast of 25″ TV unit sales by Country.
4	500	Near-term forecast of 27″ TV unit sales by Country.
5	1,000	Near-term forecast of unit demand for 25″ and 27″ Private-label sets.
6	2,000	All 25″ TV set Quality Indices by Company and Country.
7	2,000	All 27″ TV set Quality Indices by Company and Country.
8	750	Sales Representative average salaries by Company and Country.
9	250	All 25″ TV set Advertising budgets by Company and Country.
10	250	All 27″ TV set Advertising budgets by Company and Country.
11	300	Estimated R&D budgets by Company and Country.
12	300	Estimated QC budgets by Company and Country.

the Merlin Group will conduct for you, along with their fees, are presented in Exhibit 3.12. Information is available on the unit sales results of your competitors by country, the relative size of each market segment by country, and the perceived quality levels of the products you are facing in the different geographic markets.

The Merlin Group has quoted its standard rates in American dollars because it is a California-based research firm. It also must receive its payments in American dollars. To obtain its services, your company should pick the items it wants to have researched by selecting the appropriate question number(s) from those listed in your "Decision Log's Marketing Research Request" form, found in Appendix A of this manual. The Merlin Group's fees will automatically be charged to your current quarter's home country miscellaneous expense account.

PRIVATE-LABEL BIDS

One of your home country's major home electronics chains has run a private branding program of its own for a number of years. The "Kingston" brand has been very successful for the Home Electronics King chain, and it has been very competitive with the privately labeled television sets and home appliances sold by Sears and K-Mart.

Your game's global industry report bulletin board will periodically list bid requests made by the Home Electronics King chain. It will cite the number of sets they want for delivery the next quarter as well as the quality grade desired. If your firm wishes to bid for this business you must (1) enter your contract price offer in the appropriate "TV Contract Bid" spaces under "Marketing" in GBGPlayer, and (2) dedicate the required number of units under "Logistics" in the "TV Contract Distribution" form. Home Electronics King operates only in your home country market, and the chain pays for all shipping and handling charges associated with the bid. All sets are shipped from your factory and completely bypass any distribution centers or wholesalers you use in your normal distribution channel.

The winning bid will go to the firm in your industry with the lowest price who makes sets at a quality grade level that meets or exceeds that specified in the bid request. To make a reasonable profit on its privately labeled sets, Home Electronics King expects to pay a price that is significantly below what it normally has to pay its wholesale suppliers. If the price you are asking is too high for Home Electronics King's profit goals, it will refuse your offer because of these considerations. You will be notified of this decision via an announcement on your operations report.

Your firm must also guarantee the delivery of any "won" bids. If your firm has the lowest acceptable price, but fails to deliver or dedicate for shipment under "Contract Shipping" the number of sets demanded, your winning bid is cancelled and all units intended for Home Electronics King are returned to your firm's finished goods inventory for sale during the quarter. These cancelled sets cannot be reworked or retrofitted to change their current quality grade level.

THE MARKETING/PRODUCTION INTERFACE

Your company has now familiarized itself with how products are sold, distributed, and marketed in *The Global Business Game*. Your next task is to learn how to produce as economically and as reliably as possible all the products your sales representatives can sell, given the demand you have created for your products through your sales promotion efforts. It will be very difficult for you to obtain a perfect match between what can be sold and what can be produced and distributed, but you should try to come as close as possible to this ideal. A PowerPoint tutorial has been prepared for your use should you wish to review your company's distribution system. It is labeled "DistributionSystem" and can be found at the game's dedicated "Player's Resources" Web site at: http://www.swcollege.com/management/gbg/gbg.html.

For your factory or factories to run as smoothly as possible, your firm's marketers must produce fairly accurate sales forecasts while also delivering product to customers. Information obtained from the Merlin Group may be useful in providing plant management with sales estimates so they can determine how much factory capacity will be needed in the long term and how much should be produced in the short term, given temporary capacity constraints. At this time, it might be wise to develop forecasting methods that will help you to coordinate these efforts. Regardless of what you do, plant operations and marketing go hand in hand, and you must ensure that this will be a prosperous collaboration.

Chapter 4

Manufacturing Operations

Your company's manufacturing function lies at the core of your operations because your company produces television sets for sale to the consumer market. In Chapter 3, which dealt with marketing and distribution, the emphasis was on selling products and making sure they were the right products at the right price at the right time. This was a market-based or externally derived view of how a firm succeeds in the long term. In this chapter, the focus is an internal one, and the stress is on making those television sets that have sold well in the past as efficiently as possible and delivering them for distribution in adequate quantities.

Based on your company founders' design expertise and their engineering bias, your firm has attempted to obtain a strategic advantage by designing TV sets that have creative circuitry and assembling them under strict quality control standards. Rather than designing and manufacturing a television set's basic components or subassemblies, your company has put its resources into the creative application of subassemblies made by others. Given the television industry's relative maturity, which has generated a number of parts suppliers with excess capacity, and the high cost of setting up and running a subassembly factory, your firm has decided to let others produce what are near commodities within the electronics industry.

All current manufacturing operations are conducted in your home country of the United States in a wholly owned facility in Erie, Pennsylvania. The site, which was purchased for $200,000, has excellent rail and expressway connections, with additional land space readily available for plant expansions, if desired. The local labor supply is adequate for both your current and future needs, and you have obtained favorable long-term tax waivers and abatements from your local government to keep you in the area as a major employer. Your firm, nonetheless, is subject to the relatively high labor rates charged in this highly industrialized and unionized part of the country. As a hedge against these high labor rates, your company has recently purchased three automated assemblers, or automatons. These automatons are highly productive because they operate at relatively high quality control levels and require little maintenance and supervision. More important, they do not require wages and fringe benefits to make them productive, and they also increase a plant's base productivity without requiring additional space.

Despite the attractions of your Erie, Pennsylvania, site, it is also a long distance from most of your major city markets in the United States. It is even farther from your firm's potential overseas markets. Given the global and changing nature of your industry, a number of overseas manufacturing locations may be available to you if your game administrator has structured your game in that fashion. If that option is not available to you, wage/cost pressures alone on your Pennsylvania plant may require you to change how you assemble your television sets. Considering either foreign or domestic perspectives, your company may have to make a number of important decisions in this regard.

THE PRODUCTION PROCESS

Your company uses a standard method for manufacturing its sets. This is the traditional hand-tended assembly line, throughput method used in high-volume, mass-assembly factories found throughout the world. Exhibit 4.1 shows how your plant has been configured, and this is the one you have inherited from your company's previous management group, unless your game administrator or instructor has changed your company's starting position.

Under this manufacturing system, you have workers who perform their tasks within designated work stations. One side of the assembly line usually works on 25-inch sets coming down its side of the flat assembly belt. If your company also makes 27-inch sets, these sets usually come down the belt's other side. If you devote your plant exclusively to either one of these two basic sets, the spaces on both sides of the assembly line would be occupied by appropriately trained personnel. Your only constraint is that both sets cannot be simultaneously manufactured on the same side of the plant's assembly line although they can be sequentially manufactured in same-size batches.

Exhibit 4.1   Assembly Line Operations

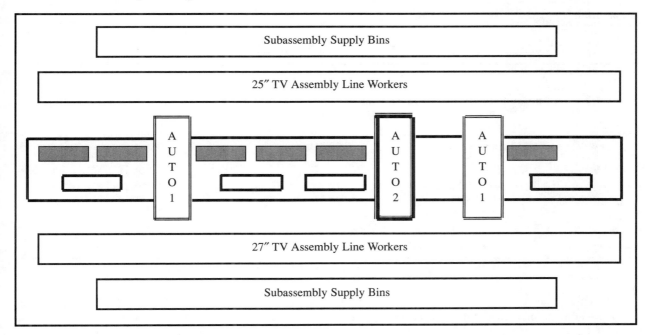

Your workers apply components to the television chassis coming down the line from two groups of subassemblies taken from supply bins placed behind them. The subassemblies involve each set's audio and visual circuits as well as each unit's cabinetry. Exhibit 4.1 indicates that 25-inch sets are more easily assembled than are 27-inch sets, as they are more closely spaced on the belt and have fewer components placed inside the chassis.

Three automatons are currently straddling your assembly belt. This indicates that your facility is operating at a relatively low level of automaticity, as it is employing two Auto1s and one Auto2. These mechanical workers, or robots, operate in humanlike fashion by sensing, through the use of bar codes and transponders, the components that must be installed in the TV chassis when it arrives at its station. As a manufacturing technology, automatons possess a degree of intelligence, require no supervision, and perform minimal maintenance operations and quality-control tests on themselves and their work. In many instances they have replaced various operations performed by workers on traditional, hand-tended assembly lines.

More automatons can be added to your line, given your line's base capacity. This *base capacity* is determined by the *line's length*. Automatons can be placed anywhere along the line, as your Auto1s and Auto2s can be programmed to perform a wide range of functions. When you are adding automatons to your assembly line, you are basically packing your given-size line with more productive nonhuman workers, thereby increasing your factory's output without changing its absolute physical size.

As more automatons are used in your assembly process, fewer and fewer line workers are required to make the same number of television sets. The number of technicians needed to reprogram your automatons, however, increases. Exhibit 4.2 (page 40) indicates the characteristics of these automatons and the number of higher-paid technicians needed to service them; Exhibit 4.3 (page 40) displays the hourly automaton technician pay scales for each country in local currencies and U.S. dollars, assuming the exchange rates shown in this manual's sample global industry report. These wage rates may change over time, given the different inflationary pressures existing in each country and the internal labor market for automaton technicians.

One technician can handle the needs of four Auto1s, but one technician can comfortably handle only three Auto2s. The Auto1s and Auto2s are progressively more flexible, with Auto2s having a higher quality-control standard and operating rate than Auto1s. When an automaton of either type is placed on an assembly line, it fills the space of two human work stations, one on each side of the line.

Exhibit 4.2   Automaton 8-hour Productivity and Required Technical Support

Automaton	Hours Generated	Technicians Needed
Auto1	32	.25
Auto2	41	.30

Exhibit 4.3   Automaton Technician Hourly Wages

Country	Hourly Wage	
	Local Currency	US$
United States	US$23.32	23.32
Mexico	Mex$16.52	1.86
Germany	€35.37	30.01
Spain	€17.28	14.66
Japan	¥2,586.45	20.05
Thailand	B77.44	1.94

Exhibit 4.4   Labor-Hour Requirements by Product

Set Size	Hours
25-inch	1.8
27-inch	2.0

As a plant manager or production scheduler, your task is to use your factory's labor-hour capacity to make television sets for shipment to distribution centers, whether those labor hours are created by human labor or the artificial labor of automatons. Exhibit 4.4 shows the total number of labor hours it takes to make each of the two set sizes you can manufacture. Given your current plant's base capacity, its length allows 140 workers to be equally split on each side of the assembly line per shift. Without automatons, your factory could produce approximately 622 25-inch television sets each working day, or 3,110 per week. You could make 560 27-inch sets per shift per day. If you were to run two full shifts, your output would almost double. Under your company's overtime option, which can run as a 25.0 percent extension of your plant's second shift, your total output could be 1,400 25-inch sets, or 1,260 27-inch sets a day. This assumes that all workers scheduled for work actually appear for work.

Your current plant, however, has three automatons. Although the space required for your automatons eliminates six laborers, the automatons increase the net productivity of your factory. As currently configured, your plant uses 134 workers, two Auto1s, and one Auto2. This configuration could theoretically generate 1,177 labor hours per shift, which would work out to 653 25-inch TVs or 588 27-inch sets if your plant was fully staffed.

WORKER SCHEDULING, VACATIONS, AND ABSENTEEISM

Before each quarter begins, your company must request the total number of workers it wants on the factory's payroll based on the types of sets to be manufactured. This is done by assigning workers by shifts to products. Your 27-inch set workers receive a higher hourly wage than that earned by your 25-inch set workers due to their greater experience and seniority. When scheduling your plant's operations, 27-inch set workers can assemble both their own sets and the simpler 25-inch sets. Workers on 25-inch sets, due to their lack of experience and skill, cannot effectively work on 27-inch sets. Although 27-inch workers can make 25-inch sets, this is not a very rational action, as you are hiring the most expensive workers to make the cheapest sets. If you actually use 27-inch workers to make 25-inch sets, certain line changeover inefficiencies will occur that lower your plant's efficiency. Inefficiencies also occur if you mix set sizes on the same side of the line.

The prevailing base wage rates for *The Global Business Game*'s six countries by set size are presented in Exhibit 4.5. The rates stated here are in local currencies and may change during the course of the simulation due to wage rate fluctuations. The prevailing factory wage rates for the countries in the business game will be regularly posted as part of your simulation's quarterly global industry reports. Based on these wage rates, and assuming that no automatons have been installed, a firm making a 25-inch television set in the United States would carry a unit labor charge of $31.61.

Exhibit 4.5 Base-Period Hourly Wage Rates by Factory Task Assignment (in local currencies)

Country	Assignment	
	25-inch	**27-inch**
United States	US$17.56	US$17.74
Mexico	Mex$11.25	Mex$11.60
Germany	€30.43	€30.73
Spain	€12.17	€12.60
Japan	¥2,212.03	¥2,444.87
Thailand	B137.75	B141.71

Exhibit 4.6 Shift 1 Charges for 27-inch Sets for Selected Countries

Country	Currency	
	Local	**US$**
Mexico	Mex$23.20	2.45
Germany	€61.46	72.44
Japan	¥4,889.74	37.90

Because different hourly wages exist throughout the world, many manufacturers have established offshore plants. Due to Germany's high hourly wages, many manufacturers have chosen not to produce their products in that country. Many German firms have sought lower-cost production sites, with a favorite European site being Spain. Using the currency rates found in the sample global industry report, Exhibit 4.6 reports the base labor costs that would apply to your 27-inch TVs if they were made in the countries shown.

While your company must schedule the number of workers it wants per product before the following quarter's run, the actual number of hours delivered may be lower than scheduled. This may be because of lost hours due to vacations, sick days, and absenteeism, or to running out of subassemblies, which would cause your plant to shut down temporarily. Vacations and authorized sick days are part of your company's wage and salary benefits plan, but absenteeism is more a function of your work crew's work ethic. Company benefits vary from country to country, as does the work ethic.

In the more disciplined and economically advanced countries of Germany and the United States, you can expect that very few workers will be unofficially absent from work. The absenteeism rate in the less developed countries of Mexico and Thailand, however, may amount to as much as 15.0 percent of the labor hours requested or scheduled.

Another factor that can cause worker absenteeism is the amount of maintenance work you budget for your factory. Equipment begins to break down and becomes dangerous to use when your maintenance budget is deficient. Under these conditions, workers who either take pride in their work or have concerns for their personal safety seek employment elsewhere and are often missing from work. In the countries of United States, Germany, and Japan, this maintenance factor is especially important. Regardless of the number of workers who actually report for work, your company must pay the wage bill on the number of workers requested, not the bill for the actual number of labor hours delivered.

These work ethic elements, along with each country's vacation and sick-day regulations, should be factored into your scheduling practices. Exhibit 4.7 summarizes the prevailing vacation and sick-day practices and behaviors your company faces. As shown, the average vacation for the types of workers your company needs in the United States lasts 4 weeks, and each worker also takes about 5 sick days a year. Absenteeism runs about 1.7 days a year. In Germany, the average vacation is 6 weeks long, and 12 sick days are authorized and usually taken. Absenteeism, however, is very low.

As an example of this factoring-in process, if you wanted to have an average of 65 workers in an American plant, you would need 70 workers on the payroll to cover all the vacations that would be taken. Looking at the German

Exhibit 4.7   Vacations, Sick Days, and Absenteeism (by country)

Country	Vacation Weeks	Sick Days	Absent Days
United States	4	5	1.7
Mexico	3	3	5.4
Germany	6	12	.2
Spain	4	4	2.0
Japan	3	5	.5
Thailand	2	4	14.0

Exhibit 4.8   Product Subassembly Requirements

	Set Size	
Group	25-Inch	27-Inch
1	8	9
2	6	7

experience, after considering the average number of sick days that would be taken per year, which amounts to 2.4 weeks, you would need to have about 3 surplus workers on hand to cover for those calling in sick. This surplus amount does not consider the number of additional workers needed to cover Germany's average 6-week vacation.

TELEVISION SET COMPONENTS AND SUBASSEMBLIES

The television sets you manufacture require two general groups of subassemblies. Both groups must be installed in each set to produce a complete unit. Exhibit 4.8 presents the number of subassemblies required by the two set sizes you can manufacture, classified by their major groupings. Your 27-inch sets, being the more complex of the two, require the greater number of subassemblies from both groups.

SUBASSEMBLY INVENTORIES

Your company has a practice of purchasing its subassembly raw materials via longtime supplier relationships developed in the very active Hong Kong market for electronic parts. In this center of activity, consolidators gather parts from Pacific Rim producers for large-lot shipments to manufacturers throughout the world. Thus, the prices they quote are FOB Hong Kong in US$, and they are bought and shipped in lots of 100 by grade and group.

If you wanted to order 522,347 units of a certain type and grade of subassembly, you would need to order 5,224 lots to obtain enough units. Make sure when you make your quarterly decision you enter the number of *lots* you want to purchase and not the actual number of subassembly units you desire. Although your subassemblies are readily available, their timely delivery is subject to the vagaries of overseas shipping.

For your plant to run full-time, it must have a complete supply of subassemblies in inventory before the quarter begins. If your plant runs out of subassemblies during the quarter, it will operate as long as it can by drawing down the supply of subassemblies available and applying them in equal proportions over the units you want manufactured. Once the subassemblies have been exhausted, your plant will shut down and all workers will be furloughed at full pay for the remaining business quarter. Due to the long shipping distances involved and your supply dealers' commitments to other customers, there is no possibility that your firm could obtain emergency shipments of any additional raw materials needed for a quarter's production run. Thus, your company should estimate as accurately as possible its subassembly requirements in advance.

Exhibit 4.9   Subassembly Lot Prices by Grade and Group (in base period US$)

Grade	Group 1	Group 2
A	168.96	579.31
B	128.80	463.45
C	115.00	403.00

handwritten annotations: GROUP B   128.80   500 × 128.80 =   7.57 × ▽ =

Exhibit 4.10   Lot Shipping Rates from Hong Kong (in base period US$)

Destination	Group 1	Group 2
North America (NAFTA)	7.57	8.43
Western Europe (EU)	13.48	15.30
Asia (APEC)	6.88	7.10

Exhibit 4.9 lists current subassembly lot prices. These prices have been quoted for the simulation's base period and are subject to change because of inflationary pressures in the producing countries and the supply and demand for the use of the same raw materials in other home and commercial electronic products. Any changes in the lot prices for subassemblies will be posted as part of the simulation's global industry report.

The shipping charges you must pay per lot to obtain these subassemblies are shown in Exhibit 4.10. These charges include handling, insurance costs, and port-of-entry processing fees. Although lots in different subassembly groups weigh about the same, Group 2's greater value and bulkier protective packaging cause them to be more expensive to ship.

SUBASSEMBLY INVENTORY CHARGES

Your subassemblies are stored in their original 100-unit lot containers, which minimizes theft, damage, and in-house handling costs. All subassemblies are also stored in high-security areas within each factory's warehouse, as these parts are easily stolen and have a relatively high unit value in spite of their small size. Thus, the cost of storing subassemblies is more a function of their monetary value and the need to have them on hand to keep assembly lines operating, than of their weight or bulk.

The majority of your subassembly storage costs lies in the insurance coverage required. This coverage, plus the extra warehouse staff needed to maintain the secured area, amounts to 1.7 percent of the value of all subassemblies on hand at the end of the previous business quarter.

SUBASSEMBLY QUALITY GRADES

Three quality grades are associated with the two groups of subassemblies used in your television sets. The quality indexes associated with these grades are displayed in Exhibit 4.11 (page 44). These subassembly grades are processed with equal efficiency by your firm's manufacturing processes. Your inventories are drawn down during the quarter's run in the proportion they are available at the beginning of the quarter, if you have a mix of grades in inventory. By mixing the grades of raw materials used in your TVs, you can have a major impact on their quality levels, their desirability, and their unit costs and subsequent retail prices.

Exhibit 4.11   Subassembly Grades and Quality Indexes

Grade	Quality Index
A	10.0
B	7.5
C	5.0

Other factors, however, also affect the physical quality of your products. These are the (1) precision of your Auto1s and Auto2s, (2) amount of training and development monies you have budgeted for factory operations, and (3) your plant's quality control budget, which screens out defective TV sets before they leave your plant. Considering only the effect of raw material grades on product quality, however, if you wanted to obtain a quality index of 10.0 for a certain run of television sets, you would have to use only Grade A subassemblies in your manufacturing process.

As an example, assuming you wanted to make 11,500 25-inch sets, the following start-of-quarter supply of raw materials would produce a group of new 25-inch TVs having a 7.27 quality index rating.

Group	Grade A	Grade B	Grade C
1	33,557	22,098	39,338
2	20,412	22,704	28,884

As a check on your mathematics, this particular run of 11,500 25-inch TVs would leave you with the following ending supply of raw materials by grade and group:

Group	Grade A	Grade B	Grade C
1	1,057	696	1,239
2	851	946	1,204

As a further check on your mathematics, the unit cost of each of your 25-inch sets would be $70.91, using the unit labor charges previously calculated for a set this size.

Unit labor cost	$31.61
Subassembly landed costs:	
Group 1, grade average	10.98
Group 2, grade average	28.32
Total	$70.91

If your firm wanted to sell to the industry's premium quality and price segment, it would have to manufacture sets using the most expensive mix of subassembly grades. Note, however, that not all consumers in all countries can afford to purchase these highly desirable sets.

STRAIGHT-TIME, SECOND-SHIFT OPERATIONS, AND OVERTIME

When making your company's production decisions, you must determine which products you want to schedule for production and on what shift(s) they should be produced. You can run partial shifts, run a complete two-shift operation, or use overtime as a 25 percent extension of the plant's second shift. The simulation will automatically assign the number of workers available from the labor pool you have requested for the quarter. You do not have to hire additional workers for any overtime operations, as the second shift's workers are held over for the hours needed to complete the production run you order.

Exhibit 4.12   U.S. Assembly Line Hourly Rates by Shift

Shift	Worker Assignment	
	25-Inch Sets	**27-Inch Sets**
First	17.56	17.74
Second	18.35	18.54
Overtime	27.53	27.81

In scheduling workers, you can assume that productivity is not constant between shifts. Traditionally your plant managers have found that the second shift is about 4.0 percent less productive than the first shift. When overtime has been scheduled, your managers have noticed an even sharper decrease in productivity, amounting to about 9.0 percent less than the second shift's productivity.

When your factory runs a second shift, a 4.5 percent labor premium is involved. The overtime hourly labor rate is 1.5 times the second shift's hourly labor rate. Because overtime is run as an extension of your second shift, the overtime labor rate is combined with the shift's 4.5 percent labor premium. Using the base labor hour rates presented in Exhibit 4.5, the hourly rates shown in Exhibit 4.12 would be incurred for various shift options in an American factory.

GENERAL ADMINISTRATION AND FACTORY OVERHEAD

Your company's general administration expenses are a function of a set of both fixed and semi-fixed expenses. The fixed component is the executive salaries you and your management group receive on a quarterly basis. This executive compensation amounts to $50,000 per quarter, or its equivalent amount, depending on your firm's home country.

Your company's semi-fixed general administration expenses entail the salaries of your plant's automaton technicians, a factory superintendent for each operating factory, a country market liaison executive for each country market in which sales are conducted or a factory is in operation, all assembly line supervisors, clerical staff, the capacity of your factory(ies) measured by its base capacity labor hours, the supervision of any plant construction, automaton installation and equipment transfers or removals, and one-time charges and security protection for any plant that has been liquidated or decommissioned. These charges apply to your Erie, Pennsylvania, plant and to any offshore operations but in equivalent local currency values and wage rates:

Country market liaison—$25,000.00/country
Factory superintendent—$38,000.00/factory
Assembly line supervision—$17,000.00/line supervisor
Automaton technicians—$23.32/hour/technician
Factory size—$20.00/base labor hour capacity
Capacity change supervision—10.0 percent of construction and/or automaton value
Equipment transfer/removal supervision—15.0 percent of equipment book value
Plant decommissioning—A one-time cost amounting to 5.0 percent of the book value being shut-down plus severance pay for the factory's superintendent and line supervisors, job counseling for automaton technicians and line workers, social costs, first-time security protection, and ongoing quarterly security patrol charges
Plant liquidation—Severance pay for the factory's superintendent and line supervisors, job counseling for automaton technicians and line workers' social indemnities owed to local government agencies and the shut-down of the factory's distribution center and sales office

WORK IN PROCESS

A nonsignificant number of units will be left unfinished at the end of each quarter because of the high speed at which your assembly line operates. Thus, your firm will have no work in process, and you can assume that all operations and production runs have been cleaned up at each quarter's end.

FINISHED GOODS INVENTORIES

During your company's operating quarter you will have created a number of units for distribution. All units left over from current production and product transfer-ins from other country and company operations, after making all sales, are gathered into a finished goods inventory account. The finished goods inventory valuation of these products is the weighted average of the mix of all products found in your inventories, regardless of their source or the originator's initial cost.

To obtain sales in other countries, your firm must transfer products from its factories to its distribution center(s). This action is not automatic. If you do not place your products in your distribution center(s), they will merely sit in temporary storage at your factories while they wait for your disposition. While sitting as finished goods on your factory floor, inventory charges are not assessed, as this is temporary in-house storage.

WARRANTY WORK

Your factory will inevitably produce a modest number of defective television sets. This is due to variances in automaton operating characteristics, the amount of supervisory and training and development attention given to your workers, and the size of your company's maintenance budget. Defects are quickly discovered by those who buy your sets. When this occurs, they return their defective sets to the retail store from which they made their purchase. If the set is returned while it is under its one-year parts warranty, the retail dealer, in turn, returns the set to the nearest country distribution center for warranty repairs. When this happens, the center absorbs the repair costs in local currency values.

Standard warranty charges are made for each returned set: $20.00 for 25-inch sets and $26.50 for 27-inch sets returned in the United States. Warranty charges in offshore distribution centers are in equivalent local currency values. No warranty charges are assessed on contract sets, as the retailer private-branding your sets performs the warranty work.

PRODUCT QUALITY

It was pointed out in Chapter 3 on marketing and marketing logistics that your company can differentiate its products both psychologically and physically. It is here, at the factory operating level, that you implement any strategies you may have for your company regarding product quality and product differentiation. This quality level is indicated as the quality index found in your operations report. The value reported reflects the weighted average of any product size category found in the firm's ending finished goods inventories.

This chapter's section on subassembly quality grades indicated a major way product quality levels are determined—through the quality mix of the components used in making your sets. A second method for improving product quality is via the mix of automatons you use, due to the tolerance or precision levels associated with each Auto1 and Auto2. A third method entails the creation and staffing of factorywide training and development programs. These programs enhance your personnel's capabilities and flexibility by training workers in new job techniques and in re-educating the technicians who program your automatons. The last way you can improve product quality is through the number of line supervisors you employ per factory. Having a greater number of line supervisors helps workers perform at optimal levels because such enlightened management techniques as quality circles can be used and closer supervision can be applied to the work as the sets are being assembled.

AUTOMATON PRECISION

Just as your automatons produce different amounts of product by set size, they also differ in their ability to produce defect-free products. Exhibit 4.13 shows that your Auto1s and Auto2s have accuracy rates that range from 94.0 percent

Exhibit 4.13   Automaton Precision Levels and Variance Rates

Automaton	Accuracy	Variance
Auto1	94.5%	±2.5%
Auto2	98.5%	±1.2%

Exhibit 4.14   Ideal Line Supervisor Control Spans

Country	Workers
United States	24
Mexico	9
Germany	26
Spain	16
Japan	29
Thailand	8

to 98.5 percent with per-type automaton variances ranging from ± 1.2 percent to ± 2.5 percent. Depending on the automaton mix in your factories, the products will be directly affected by these empirically derived machine performance ranges, given the quality grade of subassemblies used in the production process.

As an example of the interaction between subassembly grades and automaton accuracy on television set quality assume only Auto1s and Autos were used in the production process using a correct supply of Grade B subassemblies from both groups. This restriction eliminates or holds constant the effects on product quality produced by human labor inefficiencies, training and development monies and the adequacy of line supervision. Using only Auto1s the Quality Index for 25″ and 27″ TVs would be 7.09 ranging from 6.91 to 7.26. If only Auto2s were used to make the sets the Quality Index range would be 7.20 to 7.47 with an average Quality Index of 7.39.

WORK CREW TRAINING AND DEVELOPMENT

Another way you can maintain or improve the quality of your television sets is to actively engage in training and development efforts. These efforts are applied to your assembly line workers and your automaton technicians. A small, semi-fixed amount for continued work crew training is necessary for the efficient operation of your assembly operations. If your basic plant size and the number of assembly workers you have tending the line are increased, you should increase the size of this budget. Alternatively, as the proportion of your assembly operations being accomplished by automatons increases, your assembly line worker training and development budget could be decreased, and the amount you spend on automaton technician training should be increased.

In the past your firm has spent the equivalent of about US$5,000 per quarter on its American assembly line workers, regardless of the number of automatons installed. Additionally, your company has budgeted another US$5,000 per quarter for automaton technician training. When your company's training and development effort drops below a minimum level, product quality falls and the number of products returned for warranty work increases due to shoddy workmanship and disguised assembly errors.

ASSEMBLY LINE SUPERVISION

The number of line supervisors needed to oversee each factory's assembly line is related to the total number of workers hired and therefore must be controlled or supervised, tempered by the plant's automation level and the quality of the workforce being supervised. If your assembly line's operations are more labor-intensive, the level of supervision must be higher. Each country's labor force also possesses different skill levels, which severely impacts the span of control that can be comfortably exercised by a line supervisor. When the workforce is relatively untrained and undisciplined, the span of control is much narrower. Exhibit 4.15 indicates the ideal control spans associated with each country.

Exhibit 4.15   Quality-Control Inspection Programs (in US$)

Program	Sample Size	Cost	Percent Defects
A	.50%	13,000	6.0%
B	.65%	21,000	4.7%
C	.85%	36,000	1.5%

For more highly automated plants, the optimal number of line supervisors can be lower. When your factory operates a second shift, the number of line supervisors needed naturally has to double. Overtime or premium pay is not paid to line supervisors who work a plant's second shift or overtime operations. A proper ratio of line supervisors to work crews must be maintained to ensure optimum productivity. If your level of supervisors falls either significantly above or below the optimum number, product quality falls, absenteeism increases, and returns and warranty charges will also probably increase. This is because in the first case workers feel they are being too closely supervised or "hounded" by management while in the second case workers sense a lackadaisical attitude on management's part.

As an example of the effects of too little supervision on factory management's part on product quality and worker absenteeism, assume an American plant puts 223 workers on its payroll for the upcoming quarter. The ideal number of line supervisors in this case would be 4.65 [223/48 = 4.65] rounded up to five whole supervisors. Suppose, however, management hired only three line supervisors for the plant's operations. Under this condition, product quality, as reflected in the quarter's product quality index, would fall. Absenteeism would also increase, causing a decrease in the number of labor hours generated during the quarter. These effects might be of the magnitudes shown below if the plant was making only 25-inch TVs on its first shift.

Supervision Effect	Supervision Level	
	Adequate	Inadequate
Quality Index	8.41	8.11
Absentee Hours	758.20	821.36
Hours Delivered	104,051.80	103,998.64
Sets Produced	57,806	57,771

Assembly line supervision is treated as part of your company's general administration expense. Each line supervisor earns a salary comparable to the prevailing rate in the factory's country and is about 1.4 times the salary earned by automaton technicians. If your company discharges any line supervisors during a quarter, an equivalent one-time general administration charge of US$13,750 occurs for each fired line supervisor. This charge covers severance pay and job-search counseling.

QUALITY CONTROL BUDGET

In the past your company has relied on self-inspection and the precision of its automatons to ensure that you were making TV sets with adequate quality levels. Because of the greater importance of quality in product performance, however, your company has recently installed a quality control program. You have hired a quality control supervisor making the equivalent of US$10,000 per quarter and have given this person the authority to request additional monies for various new quality control programs. These programs entail drawing product samples from the assembly line for quality assurance tests, with larger budgets allowing for more thorough testing. If you want to spend less than the current US$10,000 for quality control, you can do so. With less money spent in this area, you lose the services of a full-time quality control supervisor but instead use one on a part-time basis, depending on the salary level you have budgeted.

Because your current quality control program is very new, your previous management team had not drawn any conclusions regarding the value of this effort. In theory, however, the quality control budget should increase the perceived quality of your television sets, as any off-grade sets coming down your assembly line are immediately taken off the line and never reach the marketplace. If very few of your defective products ever entered the marketplace your company's managers felt, surveys—such as the ones conducted by *Consumer Reports* and presented in Exhibit 1.2—would generate superior quality perceptions on a par with those of Sanyo and Philips Magnavox.

Your company's quality control supervisor currently holds monthly quality circle meetings, but more important, statistically controlled studies of product samples can be used to predict and control the number of products returned for warranty work. The quality or rigor of these sampling studies is determined by the size of the sample the quality control supervisor draws from current production.

Three sample-size programs have been designed by your quality control supervisor. These programs, along with their costs and the quality control standards achieved, are presented in Exhibit 4.15. For Quality Control Program A, a 0.05 percent sample of all units produced at the designated factory would be drawn, with the guarantee that about 6.0 percent of the products that are actually defective would be released for sales. This program adds US$13,000 to your company's quality control budget. If you wanted to ensure that even fewer defective products reached the market, you could employ Quality Control Program C. In this case 98.5 percent of all products reaching the marketplace would be perfect, resulting in a quality level far superior to that achieved by Toshiba. These quality control programs use destructive tests to examine the quality of the product samples drawn. Because these tests make the sets unusable, they are deducted from the total number of units available for sale and their total value at the plant's manufacturing cost is transferred to the quality control program's budget.

PLANT AND EQUIPMENT MAINTENANCE

As your factories are used over time, and the rate at which they are used intensifies, maintenance problems increase. Wear and tear is normal and to be expected. If your plant does not use many automatons, your maintenance budget naturally must be higher, as automatons maintain themselves and thereby your plant's overall maintenance needs are lower. Nonetheless, windows get broken, roofs need repair, and assembly-belt drives and bearings need periodic replacement.

Your firm should budget its maintenance monies based on each factory's rate of use, as measured by (1) the number of labor hours actually delivered, including all shifts and overtime, and (2) the proportion of those hours delivered by automatons. Exhibit 4.16 lists the recommended maintenance monies that should be allocated to each of your types of automatons. For plant maintenance in general, in each past quarter your company has been spending about US$200.00 per worker scheduled. If your maintenance budgets fall significantly below the recommended amounts, the number of labor hours available in subsequent quarters will fall, due to the equipment that has completely broken down. If this case occurs, you can recover this lost capacity only by purchasing new base capacity.

CAPITAL EQUIPMENT CHANGES

As you know from your company's history in Chapter 2, your founders think they have left you in the position to realize a number of worldwide growth opportunities. Based on their beliefs, they expect the equity value of their company to increase dramatically under your leadership. If you want to fulfill their expectations, your management group will probably want to reconfigure or expand your company's manufacturing facilities so you can produce more television

Exhibit 4.16 **Quarterly Automaton Maintenance Requirements (in US$)**

Automaton	Budget
Auto1	200.00
Auto2	450.00

sets for overseas shipments, increase the absolute size of your initial factory, or create manufacturing facilities and wholesalers in other countries if these options are available. All these strategic moves entail alterations in your company's current manufacturing site or the creation or transfer of capital from one country to another.

AUTOMATON ADDITIONS AND TRANSFERS

Through the use of automatons, you can make your company more productive or more efficient, given a similarly valued fixed investment without automatons. This can be done by three methods, either singly or in combination. Your current plant's configuration can be changed by (1) purchasing new automatons, (2) purchasing used automatons from other companies in your industry, or (3) transferring your own automatons from your home country factory to one of your own manufacturing facilities in another country.

Regardless whether you purchase new or used equipment, or transfer your own Auto1s and Auto2s between factory sites, two quarters of time are required. Additionally, for cash flow purposes, half the monies involved is dispensed or received during the first quarter of the operation and the remaining half will be dispensed or received during the second quarter of the operation. During these two quarters your general administration account will incur a charge for supervising the automaton transfer and removal that amounts to 15.0 percent of any valuation.

As a company policy, your previous management group decided that all automatons would be purchased from the same supplier. This exclusive purchasing arrangement was employed to get the best quoted prices possible and to standardize throughout the corporation the spare parts inventories and maintenance and training procedures associated with the automatons. After investigating a number of machine-tool manufacturers in Switzerland, Germany, France, Japan, and the United States, your company decided on the family of automatons manufactured by a prominent company in Turin, Italy. As part of the negotiations for the sale of its automatons, the Italian machine-tool manufacturer included as part of its price the costs of installing the automatons and the initial training of the automaton technicians who would program them. The shipping costs from Turin to your possible factories, however, are borne by your company, per the schedule in Exhibit 4.17. These shipping costs are amortized as part of the original capital investment.

The automaton purchase prices negotiated by your company's previous management group are presented in your home country's currency in Exhibit 4.18. When plant purchases are made in Spain or Germany, the transactions are paid in euros. If they are made in Mexico, Japan, or Thailand, they are made in their local currency equivalents according to the exchange rates in effect at the time of sale. Your company at the corporate level must ensure that the receiving country unit has adequate actual and anticipated funds to cover all cash flow needs associated with the equipment purchase. If not, it is possible that an overdraft may be forced on your company at its corporate level.

Another way your company can reconfigure a factory is to transfer automatons from one country's factory to a factory you own or are constructing in another country. The movement of Auto1s and Auto2s from one country to another is a unilateral action on your part and is accomplished by entering your decision via GBGPlayer's tool bar "Decision Set/Asset Transfers" drop-down menu. In this case your firm is basically "selling" equipment to itself, as this is a lateral transfer of assets. The average depreciated value of the automatons by unit and type determines the new depreciation charges subsequently incurred by the receiving country's factory and for both countries' plant and equipment balance sheet adjustments. For this transfer to be successful, the target country's plant must already be on-line or at least one quarter into its new construction.

Exhibit 4.17 Automaton Shipping Costs from Turin, Italy (in US$)

Destination	Shipping Cost
North America (NAFTA)	45,000
Western Europe (EU)	13,000
Asia (APEC)	52,750

Exhibit 4.18 Automaton Price Schedule (in US$)

Automaton	Price
Auto1	250,000
Auto2	400,000

Exhibit 4.19   Automaton Shipping Charges and Dismantling Fees (in US$)

From	Destination					
	United States	**Mexico**	**Germany**	**Spain**	**Japan**	**Thailand**
United States	—	20,000	38,000	32,000	45,000	50,000
Mexico	5,000	—	12,000	9,000	17,000	19,000
Germany	21,000	22,000	—	16,500	31,000	22,250
Spain	17,000	11,000	4,500	—	34,000	36,500
Japan	12,500	12,000	13,000	12,250	—	2,000
Thailand	7,000	6,500	6,000	5,500	1,500	—

The transfer of automatons is subject to the shipping charges and dismantling fees listed in Exhibit 4.19. Although the values used in this table are in U.S. dollars, the equivalent amount in the company's local currency will be used except for transfers between Spain and Germany, which will be in the European Union's euros.

These fees, plus the remaining depreciated book value of the automatons being transferred, are paid by the receiving unit's operation. They become part of that unit's plant and equipment and will be amortized along with the unit's other depreciable assets. The receiving unit's cash account is debited during the quarter of transfer, and the automatons are available for production one quarter later. The selling unit's cash account is credited at the beginning of the transferring quarter, with an appropriate reduction in its plant and equipment account for the value of the automaton assets that have been transferred.

As an example of this type of transaction, assume that you want to send five Auto1s and four Auto2s to a plant you have already established in Spain. The example also assumes that the automatons you are dismantling and shipping to Spain were purchased and installed in your plant in Pennsylvania five and one-half years ago. Accordingly, the combined original book value of US$3,650,000 for the automatons you are shipping has fallen to US$1,642,500, given the automaton group's depreciation at US$91,250 per quarter. Broken down by automaton type, each Auto1 is now worth US$112,500 and each Auto2 is worth US$270,000.

Automaton Type	Unit Purchase Price	
	Original Value	**Residual Value**
Auto1	250,000	112,500
Auto2	400,000	270,000

Because a dismantling and shipping charge is required for each Automaton, amounting to US$32,000 a unit, the entire transaction entails cash and asset flows amounting to US$1,930,500. The U.S. section of your NAFTA North American balance sheet's cash account would receive a credit in this amount, whereas its plant and equipment account would be debited the same amount. An opposite set of actions would occur for the Spanish section of your company's European (EU) balance sheet.

USED AUTOMATON SALES AND PURCHASES

Another method by which the factory's configuration can be changed is by purchasing used automatons from the industry's other firms. This process is initiated by informing the game administrator or instructor that you wish to either buy or sell automatons. The game administrator will post an announcement of your company's wishes on the global industry report's bulletin board. You will also find a summary of all potential and actual automaton sales and purchases, if any are in play, as part of the simulation's asset sales drop-down menu accessed through your tool bar's decision set routine.

Once the announcement has been posted, the marketplace's forces determine what next happens. You may have responses that range from little or no interest to perhaps a number of lively sessions between your firm and potential buyers or traders. If an agreement is made, it must be written as a contract between the two parties. This is done by completing the "Plant and Equipment Sale and Transfer Agreement" in Appendix G and submitting it to the game administrator for approval. The game administrator will determine whether all negotiations have been at arm's length and whether the prices charged and received reflect at least the nominal value of the assets being transferred. If the agreement is approved, the number and types of automatons will be transferred from and to the sites referenced in the agreement.

Any capital gains or losses incurred by the selling company will be costed at the time the automatons are sold These are processed through the firm's "Other Income, Capital Sales Gains/Losses" account. Because this account is the medium being employed, any gains or losses are taxed or credited at the tax rates applicable to the particular country's operations.

PLANT CONSTRUCTION AND OUTFITTING

The simplest and most straightforward way to increase a plant's production capabilities is to increase its base capacity. This is done by increasing the length of its assembly line. This lengthening allows more workers to be placed along the line.

The beginning size for any plant, whether it was the original plant in Erie, Pennsylvania, if the United States was your home country, or is a new one to be built in a foreign country, must accommodate at least thirty total workers, or fifteen workers per side of the assembly line. Your current plant can accommodate 140 workers, of which six have already been replaced by three automatons. Your original plant without automatons cost US$3,360,000 to build and outfit, requiring a capital investment of US$24,000 per worker. Added to this cost was the purchase price of the land needed by the plant along with various site preparation charges and test borings for substrata strength; city, country, and state governmental filings; and public hearings on your plant's environmental impact. The cost of the acreage needed by a typical plant in each country is presented in Exhibit 4.20. The cost of the plant's land is added to the value of your firm's plant and equipment, while the cost of the site preparation charges and governmental filings amounting to US$150,000 is added to the construction cost of any original plant. This brings your plant's total initial investment up to US$3,710,000. It is on this amount, less the value of the factory's land, that depreciation is charged. As automatons are added to a factory, they too are depreciated but on their own ten-year schedules.

One method commonly used by firms for reaching foreign markets, and for increasing their capacity, is to build new or "greenfield" manufacturing facilities in those markets. If you should do this, your company would avoid restrictive tariff charges, would benefit from any favorable labor-hour rates, and would eliminate shipping charges to the market in which the new factory was built.

The plant construction and outfitting process is straightforward but time-consuming. Before a new plant can be built, home office site-selection teams inspect a number of potential locations. After a specific site has been selected, land surveys and test borings are taken and legal clearances are obtained from local governments. If all goes well, your company can begin construction and outfitting after the land has been purchased. The entire process encompasses two quarters. Therefore, if a plant's construction began in Quarter 2, the result would be a factory that went on-line in Quarter 4.

The site selection and land surveying involved is conducted by the home country's personnel, with local personnel ensuring compliance with all local laws, ordinances, and covenants. Because this is a home office operation, these costs are about the same regardless of the country being investigated. They amount to $150,000 per plant and, as was the case with your original plant, are capitalized along with the factory's construction and outfitting cost. Your company has become very comfortable with the US$24,000 capital per worker equation, and this is the one that applies to any new plant construction or expansions initiated by your firm.

Exhibit 4.20 Land Purchase Costs and Land Sale Values (in local currencies)

Land	United States	Mexico	Germany	Spain	Japan	Thailand
Purchase cost	200,000	430,000	194,469	117,787	25,800,000	1,200,000
Sale value	345,000	500,000	197,025	144,830	23,400,000	1,000,000

As an example of the costs and depreciation rates involved in nondomestic plant construction, assume that you want to build a base eighty-six-worker plant in Mexico, and that you want to replace some of those workers by seven Auto1s and thirteen Auto2s. Exhibit 4.21 shows the costs and depreciation charges resulting from building this new factory. Note the depreciation charges on plant and equipment are on a twenty-year amortization schedule, whereas your automatons are on a ten-year depreciation schedule and that no depreciation is charged on the value of the plant's land.

When building a factory or expanding its capacity, which is done by entering the new capacity in worker units, you must anticipate the cash flows associated with these actions. For cash flow purposes, half the value of the new plant or expansion must be paid during the first quarter of construction, and the second half must be paid during the second quarter of construction. The quarterly cash needed will be automatically deducted by the simulation, and your firm's operations report will indicate "Capacity in Progress" in labor hours. Your firm's relevant balance sheet will also indicate "Capital in Progress" during any construction quarter. Once your new plant is on-line or your automatons have been installed, their value will appear as additions to your company's plant and equipment. It is at this time that depreciation charges will begin on these capacity changes.

PLANT SHUT-DOWN, CAPACITY SALES, AND TRANSFERS

You have already been advised that your firm can ship its automatons to other factories you may have already constructed or are in the process of constructing. You can also sell a plant's automatons to other firms in your industry. Both these moves decrease a plant's capacity and may indicate an attempt to reduce commitments to a home country manufacturing operation, which has strong social implications for those living in the factory's city. If this is the case, several alternatives are available: (1) temporarily idling the plant, (2) permanently decommissioning or "mothballing" it, or (3) selling off or shipping all or part of its capacity to other country units or competitors in the industry.

If the home country's base capacity is lowered, and it is being shipped to any of your firm's other foreign manufacturing sites, the actions are the same as for transferring automatons. This is a unilateral decision and does not require approval or intervention by the game administrator. When downsizing the home country's base capacity in piecemeal fashion, the plant cannot fall below one that is large enough to accommodate thirty workers, or fifteen workers per side of the line. This is because the assembly line technology cannot be housed in smaller facilities. If a plant's base capacity falls below the thirty-worker limit, as a result of your selling or transferring most of its base capacity, it must be decommissioned. Any decommissioned plant operation entails one-time charges and continuing security charges. The one-time cost amounts to 5.0 percent of the plant's remaining book value. This is a mothballing charge that covers the erection of razor-wire security fences and high-powered lighting at what remains at the factory site. The continuing charge is for a twenty-four-hour security patrol at the quarterly wage rates found in Exhibit 4.22 (page 54). All shut-down costs are charged to the country unit's general administration expense. When your firm has taken an action that decommissions a factory, this action is confirmed via a notification appearing on your firm's operations report.

Exhibit 4.21   Building a Mexican 86-Worker Base Capacity Factory with Automatons (in US$)

Item	Cost	Quarterly Depreciation
Land cost	45,431	n.a.
Site preparation	150,000	1,875
Base plant capacity (86 × 24,000)	2,064,000	25,800
Auto1s (7 × 250,000)	1,750,000	43,750
Auto2s (15 × 400,000)	6,000,000	150,000
Automaton shipping (22 × 45,000)	990,000	24,750
Construction supervision (.20 × 9,814,000)	1,962,800	n.a.
Total	12,962,231	246,175

Exhibit 4.22 Quarterly Security Patrol Costs (in local currencies)

Country	Cost
United States	US$6,249.80
Mexico	Mex$4,086.68
Germany	€10,826.18
Spain	€4,438.98
Japan	¥861,327.70
Thailand	B49,924.43

Exhibit 4.23 Unit Base Capacity Transfer Costs (in local currencies)

	Destination					
From	**United States**	**Mexico**	**Germany**	**Spain**	**Japan**	**Thailand**
United States	2,500	13,800	2,660	2,170	430,000	144,300
Mexico	5,000	2,100	820	620	163,000	138,000
Germany	21,000	15,250	770	590	295,000	64,200
Spain	17,000	7,600	300	290	324,000	67,000
Japan	12,500	8,300	870	845	1,000	5,700
Thailand	7,000	7,000	790	770	14,300	750

To reduce the plant's size, enter the amount of worker capacity and any automatons to be transferred and the countries to which the capacity is to be sent in the appropriate spaces in the "Decision Set/Asset Transfers" drop-down menu in GBGPlayer. It takes two quarters for this plant and equipment to be torn down, carted away, shipped, and installed in its new home. To minimize production disruptions caused by dismantling automatons only one of each type can be sold or transferred each quarter. Any country receiving the used capacity must already have its plant on-line, or have the plant under construction for at least one quarter. During the first quarter of this operation, the home country unit's general administration account is charged 15.0 percent of the depreciated value of the capacity being torn down in the form of equipment transfer and removal supervision. The accounting and cash flow operations associated with base capacity transfers are the same as those for transferring automatons. The cartage, shipping, and installation costs accompanying base capacity transfers are summarized in Exhibit 4.23 while the costs for transferring automatons have already been presented in Exhibit 4.19.

On occasion you may find you temporarily have too much capacity or an undesirable finished goods inventory build-up. Under these conditions it might be advisable to shut down the plant for a quarter or so until the capacity is again needed. This shut-down is accomplished by not staffing the factory with line workers, line supervisors, or automaton technicians, although plant maintenance must continue. The plant's factory superintendent is kept on payroll to manage the factory's restart if that ever occurs.

Another way to lower the firm's plant investment is to liquidate it or sell it off to the industry's other firms. If it is your desire to completely eliminate the home country's factory, it would probably be best to try to sell it to others, as severe capital losses are suffered under liquidation. Your offer to sell base capacity is handled the same way as used automaton sales. Inform the game administrator that you want to sell your plant under what proposed terms and an appropriate message will be posted on the global industry report's bulletin board. You must then wait to see what happens. While you are waiting, you can entertain any number of offers. You can also sell your capacity to more than one firm in any given quarter as long as the total capacity you wish to sell does not exceed the capacity you have available. If during the course of selling off a plant's base capacity the remaining plant falls below the thirty-worker technological requirement, the remaining portion of the plant will be decommissioned. You have the later option of liquidating a decommissioned plant if such an event occurs.

If no offers are received, or if your company receives offers it feels are unacceptable, the last option is to liquidate the plant by selling it to a salvaging operation. Do this by checking the "Liquidate Plant" box on the "Assets Transfer" drop-down menu under "Decision Set" in GBGPlayer. The plant will immediately be shut down and its line supervisors and superintendent will be dismissed with two months' severance pay. On the capital structure side, the plant is removed from the firm's books and is scrapped at 15.0 percent of its remaining valuation. This 15.0 percent is credited to the company's cash account while the remaining value is recorded as a capital loss on the home country's income statement, with the sale proceeds going to the balance sheet's cash account. No fees are associated with the physical part of the salvaging operation, as this is paid for by the salvager who is buying the plant and equipment for scrap metal. Subassemblies are purchased by a consolidator at 80 percent of their original values.

What remains is the factory's original land. This is no longer needed and is sold during the quarter. Capital gains can be expected on this sale of land originally costing US$200,000 if the United States is the home country. The same holds true except for Japan and Thailand, where land values have been falling slightly due to long-term economic weaknesses in Japan and political instability and financial failures in Thailand. Exhibit 4.20 indicates the value of the factory's land when it was purchased and its price when the country unit's plant is liquidated. The gains or losses on this value are recorded as "Other Income" and a capital sales gain/loss on the home country's income statement. The cash account receives any net proceeds from the land sale in the liquidating quarter.

SOCIAL COSTS

Any time you eliminate or eecommission a factory you are removing it as one of the city's major employers. This causes a number of "social" costs to arise. A large number of loyal workers are now out of work and need retraining and job counseling if they are to find other employment. Your firm also received a number of government-sponsored incentives to keep the plant as an employer and contributor to the area's general welfare. These incentives took the form of widening the highways leading to your plant, adding additional public transportation services, and expanding the vocational training programs conducted in the area's public schools. Since your company is reneging on various contractual and implied commitments, compensatory refunds are proper if they have been granted to your firm. The amounts involved are presented in Exhibit 4.24, where the total amounts associated with your line workers, automaton technicians, and line supervisors are levied on their number on the previous quarter's payroll.

ALMOST EVERYTHING IN PLACE

By now your company has reviewed the overall nature of its industry, have some ideas about how your markets operate, and know how your firm makes its products. Running your company successfully in a financial sense is covered

Exhibit 4.24 Plant Liquidation Social Costs (in local currencies)

Item	United States	Mexico	Germany	Spain	Japan	Thailand
Line Worker retraining/ counseling (per Worker)	US$700	Mex$500	€1,100	€350	¥90,300	B0
Automaton Technician retraining/counseling (per Technician)	US$750	Mex$550	€1,200	€375	¥92,000	B0
Line Supervisor severance (per Supervisor)	US$34,000	Mex$40,000	€28,500	€8,500	¥675,000	B0
Factory Superintendent severance	US$38,000	Mex$43,400	€31,900	€9,500	¥760,000	B0
Infrastructure refund	US$38,000	Mex$0	€0	€63,800	¥9,100,000	B370,500

in the next chapter, which deals with company finances and accounting for your company's activities and results. If you would like to be "tutored" on how various parts of your factory operates, you might wish to visit "Player Resources" at the game's Web site at http://www.swcollege.com/management/gbg/gbg.html. There you will find the following PowerPoint presentations and tutorials:

PlantOperations—Provides an overview of how labor hours are generated, how to schedule workers, calculating the plant's wage bill and the effects of quality control programs on product quality and unit costs.

Subassemblies—Covers the subassembly ordering process, shows how to calculate the correct subassembly order given forecasted production needs, examines the plant's production possibilities curve, and provides an algebraic solution for obtaining targeted product quality levels.

PlantCapacity—Reviews a typical plant's configuration, plant expansion costs and cash flows, the value of using automatons in the production process, and buying and selling automatons and any capital gains/losses associated with those actions.

Many opportunities face your firm and a number of financial moves may be necessary. These are covered in the next chapter. Even if you do not do anything dramatic, you will have to monitor the results of your many decisions. This can be done by intelligently using the financial and accounting reports prepared for you by *The Global Business Game*—or others you design for yourself once you thoroughly understand the strengths and weaknesses of the reports that have already been provided.

Chapter 5

Finance, Financial Markets, and Accounting Operations

As a member of your company's management team, you must ensure that a steady stream of money flows through all its operations. These flows are both short-term and long-term in nature. Most important, they need to be accurately anticipated if you want to make your company financially efficient. Your short-term needs will probably be filled by using funds received from your current sales, product licenses, and accounts receivables. Other short-term fund sources can come from short-term borrowing, currency exchange gains, and interest income from short-term investments.

Because your firm might compete in a number of growing markets, you may need to obtain longer-term financing for fixed plant investments and occasional foreign start-up costs. To support these efforts, you can engage in corporate bond and/or common stock sales. If your game administrator has set *The Global Business Game* to operate internationally, you will have access to several major international financial markets. Each market's operating patterns, variances, interest rates, and national risks have been incorporated in the GBG's model. In setting this financing challenge, your game administrator can choose to (1) use data from the real world's various money markets, (2) supply you with a set of quarterly data that approximates real-world conditions, or (3) freeze the money market conditions throughout the entire simulation.

If your game administrator chooses to use actual money market data in your simulation, the economic and money market indicators and data shown in Exhibit 5.1 (page 59) will be used for each of the simulation's major financial markets of New York City, Frankfurt, and Tokyo. These indicators are commonly available and are listed on a daily basis in such financial sources as Section C of *The Wall Street Journal,* and monthly in the "Monthly Survey of Interest Rates" in the *Business International Money Report*. These indicators will be updated for each quarterly run of your simulation by your game administrator, and you should take this information into account as you make your financing decisions.

You can see from reading this Player's Manual that your company has already created an integrated accounting system that is adequate for most purposes. Because this has been done, your major accounting task will be to understand the nature of the results reported each quarter and to create *pro forma income* statements and balance sheets of the types presented in Appendixes C and D. As you become more familiar with your firm's financial reporting needs, you might consider creating additional spreadsheet-based accounting information systems for yourself.

When your consolidated or home country unit enters the equity market, or any of your local operations enter the debt market, the actual interest rates charged, or the stock issue yield obtained by your firm, will vary, depending on the unit's credit rating in the current quarter. Accordingly, the debt interest rates associated with the indicators in Exhibit 5.1 present the base upon which your firm will be assessed interest rates on short-term loans or its ten-year bond issues. The range of credit ratings employed in the simulation, and their associated interest rates, are presented in Exhibit 5.2 (page 59).

COMMON STOCK ISSUES

One way to finance your company's operations is to issue common stock. This decision is indicated by entering the number of shares you wish to sell. Your firm's initial corporate charter has authorized the sale of up to 10,000,000 shares, of which 2,500,000 shares are already outstanding. This is indicated on the "Common Stock" line of your balance sheet.

Stock issues are a corporate-level or home country decision, so your company's shares are traded on the exchange that is associated with your home country's operation. This is the New York Stock Exchange for the simulation's NAFTA countries of Mexico and the United States, the Frankfurt Stock Exchange for the EU countries of Germany and Spain, and the Tokyo Stock Exchange for the APEC countries of Japan and Thailand.

Exhibit 5.1 Data Sources for Money Markets and Financial Activities

Indicator	New York	Frankfurt	Tokyo
Ninety-day short-term loan	Three-month Treasury bill deposit	Three-month eurodollar	Money market rate
Ten-year bonds	U.S. Treasury bond	U.K. government bond	Japanese government bond
Stock market activity	Dow-Jones Industrial Average	Frankfurt DAX-30	Tokyo Nikkei 225

Exhibit 5.2 Credit Ratings and Debt Interest Rates

Credit Rating	Ten-Year Bond Rate	Short-Term Loan
AAA	Bond Rate + 1.0 point	Short-Term Rate
AA	Bond Rate + 1.5 points	Short-Term Rate + 3.0 points
A	Bond Rate + 2.5 points	Short-Term Rate + 7.5 points
B	Bond Rate + 6.0 points	Short-Term Rate + 15.0 points
C	Bond Rate + 8.5 points	Short-Term Rate + 24.0 points

Your firm's stock is sold through an underwriter, who ensures that all the shares you offered will be sold—although perhaps at a steep discount, if necessary. The underwriter's fee, or commission for underwriting your issue, is a flat $15,000, plus 1.5 percent of the stock issue's total market value. The cash proceeds from the issue, and the share price at which your stock was sold, will vary depending primarily on the issue's size, because the issue temporarily dilutes your shareholders' claims on potential stock dividends. For cash flow purposes, your firm receives the proceeds of the stock sale one month into the issuing quarter.

When setting the initial price for your stock offering, your underwriter takes into consideration the stock's value in the previous quarter. Thereafter, the forces of the equity capital marketplace take over. It is almost certain that your stock's price will be discounted, although the exact amount of discounting that will occur cannot be predicted exactly. The net proceeds from the stock sale, after the stock's dilution and the payment of all underwriting fees, are added to consolidated's cash account and to owner's equity during the quarter of issuance. If your issue sells above its nominal $1.00 par value, the surplus above par is added to your paid-in capital. If your stock issue sells for less than its par value, the issue's decrement below par is subtracted from retained earnings. Exhibit 5.3 provides an example of the actions and balance sheet changes associated with a stock sale of 750,000 shares of common stock.

The results presented in this exhibit and in Exhibit 5.4 were generated by a spreadsheet program that emulates your game's stock market and tries to take out some of the guesswork your company may have to engage in when dealing with stock transactions. This program labeled "STOCKS" is available to your game administrator under "Game Administrator Resources" on the game's Web site. You might ask that it be downloaded for your company's use in future quarters.

TREASURY STOCK PURCHASES

Your company can purchase its shares on its own account. This action, which is indicated by entering the number of shares you wish to purchase, or "retire," will temporarily increase the value of all remaining outstanding shares, as this operation's temporary effects are the opposite of those associated with a stock issue. To guard against stock price manipulation on your part, your board of directors has placed two limitations on your making Treasury stock actions: the number of shares outstanding cannot fall below 2 million at any time, and retained earnings must always be positive. The simulation will automatically void any Treasury stock action whose results would cause either of these conditions to be violated.

When Treasury stock is purchased, shareholders sell their shares at a premium. This premium is at least 9.0 percent above its most recent quote. Accordingly, a stock that was listed at $24.37 a share on the last day of Quarter 3 would be purchased by your firm in Quarter 4 at a price that would be not less than $26.56. When such a purchase is

Exhibit 5.3   A Stock Sale Example

Quarter 1 shares outstanding	2,500,000
Quarter 1 stock price	$18.50
Market value of shares outstanding (18.50 × 2,500,000)	$46,250,000
Shares issued in Quarter 2	750,000
Stock price after dilution effects ($46,250,000/3,250,000)	$14.23
Issue gross proceeds (14.23 × 750,000)	$10,672,500
Less brokerage fees:	
Flat fee	$15,000
Commission	$160,088
Issue net proceeds	$10,497,413
Proceeds to common stock	$750,000
Proceeds to paid-in capital	$9,747,413

Exhibit 5.4   A Treasury Stock Purchase Example

Quarter 3 shares outstanding	4,730,000
Quarter 3 stock price	$24.37
Shares purchased in Quarter 4	500,000
Estimated Treasury stock price	$26.56
Stock purchase cost ($26.56 × 500,000)	$13,280,000
Cost from common stock	$500,000
Cost from paid-in capital	$12,780,000

consummated, your firm's cash account is debited the entire cost of the stock purchases, with your common stock account debited the par value of the shares retired and any excess above par deducted from your paid-in capital account. Exhibit 5.4 provides an example of these Treasury stock actions.

DIVIDENDS

Your shareholders are vitally interested in your company's stock performance, as well as the dividend payout policies you have created for yourself. Thus, you may wish to issue dividends periodically, given other financial considerations your company faces. All dividends are issued on a per share basis.

The total value of any quarterly dividend should not exceed your firm's projected total retained earnings for the dividend quarter. Declarations that are greater than retained earnings are basically liquidating dividends and will be voided by the simulation. This type of dividend is also frowned upon by your stockholders, who wish to see their company continue as a viable enterprise for many years to come.

DEBT ISSUES

Your firm can also cover its cash requirements through various combinations of debt financing. This is in the form of short-term debt, long-term debt, and cash transfers from the proceeds of any debt action. These debt instruments can be (1) ninety-day, short-term loans obtained from commercial banks in each marketing area's major commercial market and (2) ten-year bonds. Should your overall consolidated operations experience a cash shortfall during any operating quarter, the simulation will automatically issue an overdraft, which is unplanned debt financing of a very expensive and undesirable form.

OVERDRAFTS

This is basically a distress loan. It is the least attractive and most costly way to finance your company's business. During any particular quarter, an area operation of yours might become technically insolvent. Should this occur, the simulation will first attempt to cover the cash shortfall from idle cash available at your company's consolidated level. If cash is available, consolidated will automatically transfer the necessary funds to the deficient local operation without a penalty to the technically bankrupt operation. If cash is insufficient at the consolidated level, an overdraft loan will be obtained by consolidated for each affected local operation, with cash disbursements automatically made to them during the quarter to cover any shortfall.

Because you exhausted all your firm's internal capital sources to arrive at the point that requires an overdraft, and your company has been unable to forecast its cash flow needs accurately, the cost of an overdraft is very high. The rates for consolidated's overdraft borrowings are about 24.0 percentage points above the prevailing ninety-day short-term loan rate available in its home financial market. In most applications of this simulation, your company's home market financial center is New York City.

The simulation will automatically pay off your company's overdraft during the following quarter. It does this by deducting from your firm's following quarter's cash flow the total amount of the overdraft plus the overdraft's interest payment for the quarter. Consequently, to maintain your company's solvency in the payoff quarter, you must plan for this "payment." While your overdraft loan is outstanding, both the principal and interest due appear as liabilities on your consolidated and country/market balance sheets.

As an example, assuming a cash flow shortfall of US$147,913 and the short-term rate for the United States, the current quarter would incur a liability of US$162,150 (147,913 × [8.50 + 30.0]/4). This amount would be taken from your company's cash flow in the following quarter, with the interest charge of US$14,237 appearing on that quarter's consolidated and country/market income statements.

NINETY-DAY SHORT-TERM LOANS

Short-term debt may be obtained by any one of your local operations within the constraints of its credit rating, past cash management experience and current ratio. If your ninety-day loan request is granted, the entire amount arrives during the borrowing quarter with the loan repaid the following quarter. The interest payment on the loan should be anticipated as it is paid in the current quarter. The repayment of this loan does not have to be entered, as the simulation automatically pays off the loan and its associated interest in the following quarter out of your company's operating cash flow. You must, of course, plan for this cash removal when making your quarter's financial plans.

TEN-YEAR BONDS

Your company can issue callable ten-year bonds in even $1,000 amounts. The interest rate on your bonds depends on (1) the yield rates on comparable ten-year bonds in the world's major money markets, (2) your firm's credit rating, and (3) your company's debt-to-equity ratio.

To enter the bond market, your company enters the dollar amount of the bonds to be sold in even $1,000s. You will receive the bond issue proceeds during the issuing quarter, with the bond's first interest payment due in the same quarter. Any number of bonds, or the value of bonds, can be outstanding at any given time—your firm needs only to service them, that is, pay their required interest each quarter.

When bonds are outstanding, their total face value is listed as a liability, and the interest expense for that quarter appears as an interest charge on your income statement. Exhibit 5.5 provides an example of a bond issue of US$450,000 placed in the New York City money market, when the company had an A credit rating and U.S. Treasury bonds had a 5.67 percent yield. The results shown here were generated by a spreadsheet program labeled "BONDS" that is available

Exhibit 5.5   A Bond Offering Example

U.S. Treasury Bond Rate	5.67%
Unit's Credit Rating	A
Bond Interest Rate	8.17%
Bond Issue Amount	US$450,000
Bond Liability	US$450,000
Bond Discount	US$24,750
Quarterly Interest Payment	US$9,191
Annual Cash Outflow	US$36,765

to your instructor or game administrator. While it is not completely accurate, it can give your firm a better idea of the proceeds and true costs of bond issues. You might ask your game administrator to make it available to your company.

In issuing your corporate bonds, it is very likely the proceeds will be less than the bond's face value. Discounts will occur and this amount of discounting occurs naturally and is charged as a one-time cost to your interest expenses. In subsequent quarters the only interest charges you incur are those needed to service the bonds that are outstanding.

There is no restriction on the amount of total outstanding bonds your firm can possess at any time. No new issue, however, can be larger than its home country unit's owner's equity or its current assets less its current liabilities. Should these restrictions not be met, the bond issue will fail and your firm will be accordingly notified of this failure on its operations report. It is also very likely that subsequent bond offerings will fail for a number of quarters after a country unit earns a C credit rating.

CALL OPTION

Your bonds feature a call option by which you can retire all or any part of their total value at any time. This option is exercised by entering the monetary value of the bond amount to be called or retired. When making this retirement, a call premium of 7.5 percent is levied on the amount being called, and this premium is charged to your firm's interest account for the quarter's call. Thus, if US$150,000 of a US$400,000 outstanding amount of bonds were called, your balance sheet's cash account would be debited US$161,250, your income statement's interest account would be debited US$11,250, and your total bond liability would fall to US$250,000. The spreadsheet program available to your game administrator labeled "BONDS" also deals with bond calls.

CASH TRANSFERS

Due to the borrowing power of different company units, and variances in interest rates associated with your firm's major money markets, you may wish to transfer cash between any local operations you may have. This can be done to handle temporary cash flow needs, allow a local operation to make short-term investments in its own money market, or pay for plant construction and equipment transfers.

These transactions are entered as cash "from" and cash "to" amounts from "donor" units and "receiving" unit(s) in the country's local currency. The country operation providing the funds is the transferor or "donor" and the country operation receiving the funds is the transferee or "receiver." The total value of the cash out-transfers must naturally equal the total value of the cash in-transfers. You should plan each country unit's financial needs just as for your home country unit. If a country unit experiences a technical insolvency during the quarter, the simulation will automatically transfer funds from your home country to cover the cash shortfall. This action will cause the country unit's credit rating to fall to a C level. Repeated shortfalls will cause your home country's credit rating to be damaged, as such deficiencies indicate your firm lacks adequate financial controls.

Exhibit 5.6 Simplified Income, Value-Added, and Dividend Tax Rates

	Country					
Tax	**United States**	**Mexico**	**Germany**	**Spain**	**Japan**	**Thailand**
Income	47.0%	50.0%	73.4%	35.0%	45.0%	35.0%
VAT	0.0%	15.0%	15.0%	12.0%	15.0%	20.0%
Dividend	0.0%	35.0%	30.0%	10.0%	20.0%	20.0%

INCOME TAXES

Because you are an international corporation, your earnings are subject to the varying taxation policies of the federal and local governments within which your units operate. All countries impose general taxes on a unit's total income, and value-added taxes may apply to varying degrees from country to country.

Exhibit 5.6 presents the income tax rates applicable within each country at the beginning of your simulation. These rates combine federal taxes with any local taxes. These taxes are paid on a quarterly basis, and the simulation automatically collects them from your firm's cash flow. Should an operating unit experience losses during a quarter, the amount of those losses is carried for a three-year period and will be used to offset, or act as a tax credit against, profits or earnings made in subsequent quarters.

VALUE-ADDED TAXES

Many countries, as a hidden and additional source of easily collected revenue, levy value-added taxes (VATs) on products manufactured within their borders. These taxes can be somewhat complex and confusing. *The Global Business Game* simplifies the assessment and collection of VATs by applying the country's particular VAT rate to the country unit's product sales less the value of all subassemblies found in the units sold in the quarter. All VATs are automatically collected from each country unit's cash flow and gross revenues to result in the net revenues actually generated by the country unit.

DIVIDEND TAXES

Many countries tax the dividends or excess capital foreign subsidiaries remit to their overseas owners. The politics of this action are to encourage foreign investors to keep their capital in the country for reinvestment purposes rather than remitting it at a heavy discount to the company's home country. Exhibit 5.6 displays the dividend tax rates being used by various nations within the simulation to accomplish this purpose.

When an overseas country unit forwards all or any portion of its retained earnings to its home country headquarters, that amount will be taxed according to the applicable dividend tax rate. As an example, if your German unit had retained earnings of €205,147 and wanted to send €100,000 of that to consolidated's retained earnings for its own dividend declaration needs, €30,000 would be taxed away, with the remaining €70,000 going to the home country's retained earnings.

THE EURO AND THE EURO ZONE

A major step in accomplishing the long-held dream of turning Western Europe into a single economic entity occurred on January 1, 1999. On that date, twelve European countries locked their national currencies to the new euro. Henceforth the exchange rates between the euro zone's countries were irrevocably fixed against each other and against the euro. At the time, however, the euro was a virtual currency not in circulation. The euro zone's countries were allowed to use both their national currencies and the euro internally until January 1, 2002, although all bond and equity operations, as well as international trade, was conducted in euros. Thereafter the only currency in circulation was the euro itself, which came in notes of 5, 20, 50, and 100 euros and coins of 1, 2, 5, 20, and 50 cents. When the euro went into circulation 14.9 billion bank notes and 52.0 billion coins were distributed through each nation's retailers, post offices, and private banks. If placed end to end, the notes could have gone to the moon and back 2 1/2 times and the weight of the coins would be equal to twenty-five Eiffel Towers.

All major European corporations began converting their accounting systems and financial portfolios well before January 1, 1999. *The Global Business Game* implements the European Union's complete conversion to the euro and states the currency values between and within Spain and Germany in euros rather than in marks or pesetas. Thus, you should think in euros when setting prices and determining costs for Spain and Germany. Because the exchange rates between Spain and Germany are now frozen, no exchange rate gains and losses can occur due to business transactions between those two nations. Exchange rate gains and losses *can* occur, however, between business done in euros versus American dollars, Mexican pesos, Japanese yen, and Thailand baht. At the beginning of 1999 the euro was valued at about $1.18 to the American dollar but it quickly fell and has historically been trading at about 84 cents to the dollar.

EXCHANGE RATE RISK

Your company's previous management group has required that all local profits and losses be converted into the home office's currency. This allows for standardized financial comparisons. Your game administrator will determine your company's home country before the simulation begins, as this establishes the base currency employed. Assuming your company's home office is in the United States, the relevant currency would be the U.S. dollar.

Any time a nation's currency changes in value relative to that of other nations, gains and losses on the exchange or conversion of those currencies will occur. If the U.S. dollar falls in value relative to another currency, the American home country company realizes exchange rate losses. If the U.S. dollar rises in its relative value, the American company receives exchange rate gains. These effects can be substantial if one of the currencies is especially volatile and a large volume of sales is made in that currency. The sum of all currency gains and losses are considered additions or subtractions from your reported profits and corporate-level retained earnings, therefore affecting your firm's owner's equity and the amount of dividends you can pay your shareholders.

To illustrate the effects of currency fluctuations on profits and intercompany comparisons, assume that the currency and exchange values shown in Exhibit 5.7 were in effect for Quarters 3 and 4 for the United States, Mexico, and Japan. Between the two periods shown, U.S. dollars rose in relation to Mexican pesos 0.1754 points, or 2.04 percent [(8.7850 - 8.6096)/8.6096) = 0.0204]. U.S. dollars in relation to Japanese dollars fell 4.01 points, or 3.1 percent [(125.50 − 129.41)/125.40) = 0.031] in value.

Exhibit 5.7   Sample Currency Rate Changes by Country

Quarter	U.S. Dollars	Mexican Pesos	Japanese Yen
		Country and Currency	
3	1.00	8.6096	129.41
4	1.00	8.7850	125.40

Now, let us assume that the following operating profits were obtained by your company's operations in Quarter 4 in the United States, Mexico, and Japan.

Proxy Income Statement in Local Currencies

Global Industry A Firm 1 MagnaArgus Corporation Quarter 4

	United States (US$)	Mexico (Mex$)	Japan (Yen)
TOTAL REVENUE	105,437	75,656	1,376,647
EXPENSES	102,001	68,546	1,174,692
OPERATING PROFIT	3,436	7,110	201,955

Converting Mexico's and Japan's local currencies into American dollars at the Quarter 4's exchange rates produces the following consolidated and country-related exchange rate gains and losses:

Proxy Income Statement in Home Office Currency

Global Industry A Firm 1 MagnaArgus Corporation Quarter 4

	United States (US$)	Mexico (US$)	Japan (US$)	Consolidated (US$)
TOTAL REVENUE	105,437	8,612	10,978	125,027
EXPENSES	102,001	7,803	9,368	119,172
OPERATING PROFIT	3,436	809	1,610	5,855
Exchange Gain/Loss		+ 16	−49	− 33

Exchange rate gains were recorded on Mexico's operations between Quarters 3 and 4 because the value of the American dollar rose in relation to the Mexican peso. This gain was US$16,000 after rounding, as it took fewer American dollars to convert Mexico's Quarter 4 earnings into dollars. Because the value of the American dollar fell in relation to Japan's yen between the two quarters, exchange rate losses amounted to about US$49,000 after rounding. This resulted in a net exchange loss of $33,000.

SHORT-TERM INVESTMENTS

Your company has two other nonoperating revenue sources in addition to selling automatons to other firms in your industry. These sources are revenues from the sale of patent rights and their accompanying royalty payments and the proceeds from locally placed short-term investments.

To make a short-term investment for an operating quarter, you designate the monetary value that is to be placed in each country's respective three-month, short-term money market. This amount is immediately withdrawn from your company unit's cash flow at the beginning of the quarter, and returns to your unit's cash account at the beginning of the following quarter. The interest income is collected during the current quarter. The interest rate or yield on this investment will be that of the ninety-day short-term money rate found in the money markets of New York City, Frankfurt, and Tokyo.

MONEY CIRCLES AND HEDGING

In prior years in the world of international commerce, firms often either capitalized on the slow pace of international currency transactions or attempted to protect themselves from wild currency fluctuations. In the former case, various firms would create money circles. These circles took advantage of the "float" or long time it took banks to reconcile their international currency accounts. In the latter case, firms felt it was useful to hedge their currency activities, especially for those associated with countries experiencing large currency valuation swings.

Through the advent of electronic reporting and electronic money transfers, the delay or lack of information that made these activities possible or lucrative in the past are not as important as before. Thus your firm cannot create a money circle, nor would it be useful to engage in hedging operations.

ACCOUNTING AND CASH FLOW OPERATIONS

The accounting system created by your company a number of years ago planned on having multiple revenue and cost sources from both its own country's operations and those overseas. In this regard the accounting statements consist, in their most elaborate form, of three separate global area reports, whose results are gathered and summarized into a consolidated report. Each area report, in the form of global area reports, presents the results from the two countries where business can be conducted in each economic zone.

This manual has previously described the nature of every item in the simulation's income statements, balance sheets, industry report, and operating statements. The present section describes the various accounting procedures used in the game, starting with your company's income statement. Many income statement accounts are budgeted each quarter—such as advertising, training and development, and research and development. These are not covered, as the income statement merely repeats your decision entry and has already been covered in earlier chapters. Instead, the more abstract cash flow implications of various entries and accounts are presented subject to the accounts receivable and accounts payable operations presented in Exhibit 5.8.

GROSS RECEIPTS

This account summarizes all revenue associated with the sale of television sets. Included in these receipts are any VATs assessed by a federal government. You must rebate this VAT to each country's tax collector. This is not a manual entry on your part, as these funds are automatically remitted to the federal government(s) involved. Thus the value of the VAT is subtracted from gross receipts to produce the net sales or operating revenue produced by your company. Approximately 80.0 percent of net sales are collected during the current quarter, with the remaining amount going to accounts receivables for collection the following quarter.

OTHER INCOME

Because your company has been defined as a manufacturer and seller of television sets, income from any other source(s) must be considered as nonoperating or extraordinary income. The three items in this account category are pure cash inflow by the end of the quarter, although your firm *could* take a book loss on the sale of any of its land, plant, and equipment, which would be charged against current earnings.

Exhibit 5.8   Summary of Cash Flow Operations

Accounts Receivable	20.0 percent of net sales and operating revenue collected next quarter. All revenues associated with "Other" nonoperating income is collected during the quarter
Accounts Payable	10.0 percent of factory worker wages for the quarter is paid next quarter
	25.0 percent of subassembly purchases
	30.0 percent of general administration expenses
	30.0 percent of sales representatives' base salaries and commissions
	50.0 percent of any new plant and equipment expenses during construction or expansion

COST OF GOODS SOLD

Your company operates under the standard weighted cost inventory method. The unit value of each of your company's three products is the weighted value per unit of the pool of (1) units drawn from any finished goods held over in inventory from previous quarters and (2) the current quarter's unit production costs and volumes. No LIFO (Last In, First Out) or FIFO (First In, First Out) option is available to your company. The value of the raw materials or Subassembly portion of each product's valuation is determined by the weighted average cost of the pool of raw materials from which your television sets are assembled. About 90.0 percent of your firm's production costs associated with worker wages are current quarter cash outflows, with the remaining 10.0 percent portion becoming an accounts payable item due the following quarter.

If tariffs are being levied on the sale of imported products by a particular host nation, these charges are added to the country unit's cost of goods sold at this time. These tariffs act to increase the cost of any products you sell in the host country, which are not produced locally, and you should consider these tariffs when setting the prices of your television sets.

GENERAL ADMINISTRATION

This is a collection of executive compensation, supervisors' wages, technician salaries, market liaison managers (if you are running any foreign operations), new construction supervision when required, an overhead assessment based on plant size, and any one-time and continuing charges associated with plant liquidations and decommissionings. Approximately 70.0 percent of this expense is a current cash outflow, with the remaining portion an accounts payable.

DEPRECIATION

This is a noncash expense, with general plant and equipment being depreciated on a twenty-year, straight-line schedule. Automatons are a special category of equipment subject to high economic obsolescence and are accordingly depreciated on a ten-year, straight-line schedule. These assets begin their depreciation once they have been installed and have become a working asset. They are listed as capital in progress while going through the installation and construction process.

INTEREST CHARGES

Any short-term loans or bonds held by your company were contracted for in a previous quarter. Accordingly, the interest charges associated with them are current quarter cash outflows. Your short-term loans, plus their interest charge, are automatically paid off by the simulation so you should accordingly anticipate this cash outflow requirement.

Overdrafts incurred by firms are not anticipated but are forced on a company that is technically insolvent during the operating quarter. In this regard the amount of the overdraft, plus its interest charge, is a cash outflow element that must be planned on by the company for the following quarter.

INCOME TAXES

Income taxes are assessed at the simplified and combined federal and local rates presented in Exhibit 5.6. These taxes are collected quarterly and therefore are a current cash outflow item. If your firm has negative profits for the quarter, a negative income tax amount will appear on your firm's income statement, and your retained earnings will be subsequently debited by the entire amount of the quarter's loss. This negative tax is a tax credit, which will be held in your company's records to act as a deduction from any future profits your firm earns within the next three years.

CAPITAL IN PROGRESS

This account sums the value of all monies associated with the construction of new plant and equipment, the expansion of current plant capacity, and the interfirm and intrafirm transfer of base capacity and automatons. The values recorded here for intrafirm base capacity and automaton sales will be the amounts agreed upon by the parties involved and duly recorded and approved by the game administrator on the appropriate "Plant Capacity and Automaton Sale Agreement" form found in Appendix G. The amount for new automaton purchases by automaton type is at the rates posted in Exhibit 4.18's automaton price schedule. New plant construction, or plant line expansion, will be at the rate of US$24,000 per worker as measured in units of base capacity. Thus, if you wanted to build a plant that could be staffed by twenty more line workers, you would have to spend US$480,000 on that facility plus incurring construction supervision costs amounting to US$96,000 for the two construction quarters.

Any setup or transportation charges associated with capacity expansions or base capacity and automaton transfers are immediately included in the cost, and the entire amount, from the quarter in which expansions are contracted, is depreciated at the rate applicable to the technology being depreciated. One-half of the cash flow cost of such an operation would be taken from your cash account or any other concurrent source of cash. The full amount of the action would appear on your balance sheet as capital in progress, and that capital would start being depreciated once it had been completely installed. The other half of the action's required cash flow would come from cash sources you provide during the following quarter's activities.

RETAINED EARNINGS

This residual item can be used for internal funding purposes or can be the source of dividend declarations. For offshore units it is an amount that is subject to transfer to your firm's home country for use at that site. If any of these retained earnings are sent to your home country, they are subject to existing dividend taxes. This tax is a current cash outflow item and must be anticipated by your operating unit before the retained earnings transfer is made.

ACCOUNTING AND CASH FLOW OPERATIONS

The income statements, balance sheets, and operations reports generated by *The Global Business Game* summarize the results produced by the many decisions you will make over the game's duration. To help you understand these reports, and to help you see how the results presented in the game's reports are created, a number of sample forms and printouts have been prepared. The materials presented in this section are for illustrative purposes only. The decisions that produced these results, as well as their underlying scenarios, do not necessarily represent the best strategies that could have been pursued or the game that has been prepared for you by your game administrator. In this example we are examining the activities of Firm 1, MagnaArgus Corporation and its overall and country unit results for Quarter 4, 2003. They have been put into a combined spreadsheet form using the cut and paste feature available to you in GBG-Player for greater viewing ease (Exhibits 5.9 and 5.10 on pages 68 and 69).

The company has made a number of tactical, short-term decisions as well as two major, strategic, long-term decisions. It has built a fairly large plant in Japan from which it is attempting to make high-quality sets for the Japanese and German markets. In the United States it has been emphasizing the sale of 27-inch television sets. The firm is not trying to be innovative, as its research and development budget is fairly small, as is also the case for its quality control and training and development budgets. Its German operation is a fledgling one and has not yet turned a profit.

Exhibit 5.9   MagnaArgus' Consolidated Income Statement

Year 2003 Quarter 4
Firm 1 - MagnaArgus Corporation

	US$ Consolidated	US$ U.S.	Euro Germany	Yen Japan
Revenues:				
Gross Revenues	19,209,486	11,586,975	765,191	866,530,612
Value-Added Tax	716,323	0	79,532	80,391,596
Net Sales	18,493,163	11,586,975	685,659	786,139,016
Other Income:				
Capital Sales Gains/Losses	0	0	0	0
Investment Income	0	0	0	0
Licenses	0	0	0	0
Non-Operating Income	0	0	0	0
Total Revenue	18,493,163	11,586,975	685,659	786,139,016
Expenses:				
Cost of Goods Sold	10,609,369	5,978,872	349,135	542,186,520
Advertising	30,433	13,000	9,560	916,000
General Administration	354,379	267,379	0	11,082,060
Sales Offices	937,632	430,000	458,040	2,154,000
Distribution Centers	737,850	355,640	264,596	12,576,853
Wholesale Operations	1,167,948	582,762	545,697	70,400
Sales Force Salaries	327,123	192,268	16,346	14,947,012
Trainees	9,100	9,100	0	0
Training and Development	22,971	13,000	4,500	656,000
Inventory Charges	268,692	204,183	0	8,217,087
Shipping	767,829	227,058	84,983	57,285,858
License Fees	0	0	0	0
Research and Development	5,000	5,000	0	0
Quality Control	13,000	13,000	0	0
Depreciation	107,625	69,750	0	4,824,518
Maintenance	102,328	48,850	0	6,812,000
Interest Charges:				
Overdrafts	0	0	0	0
Short-Term Loan	0	0	0	0
Bonds	0	0	0	0
Miscellaneous	0	0	0	0
Total Expenses	15,461,279	8,409,863	1,732,858	661,728,308
Income Before Taxes	3,031,884	3,177,112	-1,047,198	124,410,708
Income Tax	1,109,265	1,493,243	-768,643	55,984,819
Dividend Tax	0	0	0	0
Net Income	1,922,619	1,683,870	-278,555	68,425,890

Exhibit 5.10 MagnaArgus' Consolidated Balance Sheets

Year 2003 Quarter 4
Firm 1 - MagnaArgus Corporation

	US$ Consolidated	US$ U.S.	Euro Germany	Yen Japan
Assets:				
Cash	44,276,551	43,742,323	89,636	55,817,460
Accounts Receivable	3,698,633	2,317,395	137,132	157,227,803
Tax Credit	1,523,780	0	1,422,296	0
Short-Term Investments	0	0	0	0
Licensed Patent(s)	0	0	XXX	XXX
Due From Country Unit(s)	XXX	9,066,539	XXX	XXX
Inventories:				
Subassemblies	8,925,953	5,055,656	0	492,998,413
Finished Goods	0	0	0	0
Goods in Transit	210,990	0	0	26,875,952
Total Current Assets	67,702,446	60,181,914	1,649,064	732,919,629
Capital In Progress	0	0	0	0
Plant and Equipment	7,977,544	4,745,000	0	411,761,400
Less Depreciation	1,596,750	1,521,000	0	9,649,035
Total Fixed Assets	6,380,794	3,224,000	0	402,112,365
Total Assets	74,083,240	63,405,914	1,649,064	1,135,031,994
Liabilities and Owner's Equity:				
Accounts Payable	2,215,722	1,139,447	4,904	136,426,743
Overdraft	0	0	0	0
Due to Home Country	XXX	XXX	2,199,439	854,740,988
Short-Term Loan	0	0	0	0
Total Current Liabilities	11,282,261	1,139,447	2,204,342	991,167,731
Bonds	0	0	0	0
Total Liabilities	11,282,261	1,139,447	2,204,342	991,167,731
Stockholder's Equity:				
Common Stock	8,400,000	8,400,000	XXX	XXX
Paid-In Capital	49,195,833	49,195,833	XXX	XXX
Retained Earnings/Deficit	5,205,145	4,670,634	-555,279	143,864,263
Exchange Gains/Losses	0	0	XXX	XXX
	62,800,978	62,266,467	-555,279	143,864,263
Total Liabilities and Owner's Equity	74,083,240	63,405,914	1,649,064	1,135,031,994

Thus it appears MagnaArgus is implementing a strategy of market development in Germany and Japan combined with a market penetration strategy in the United States. Its generic strategy is one of focused differentiation because it is trying to make high-quality 25-inch sets for Germany and Japan and medium-quality 27-inch sets for the United States.

INCOME STATEMENT RESULTS

MagnaArgus Corporation had net sales at the consolidated level of $18,493,163. Value-added taxes in the amount of €79,532 and ¥80,391,596 were respectively collected in Germany and Japan. There were no other income sources for Firm 1, such as the sale of plant and equipment, product licenses, or short-term investments.

Currently, Germany's products are made in Japan with its start-up funds coming from the United States. Accordingly, Germany's operations incurred none of the expenses typically associated with manufacturing operations and they were exclusively carried by Japan's factory. Thus MagnaArgus' German unit is primarily a marketing organization and fulfills this role by absorbing numerous shipping charges and spending most of its monies maintaining, operating, and supervising its marketing channels.

Firm 1's American and Japanese activities, however, were much more diverse. These operations engage in manufacturing, incur all the costs associated with operations management, and run their own marketing functions. The net result of these activities resulted in an American-based profit of $1,683,870 and a Japanese profit of ¥68,425,890. There were no currency translation gains or losses between Quarters 3 and 4, 2003.

BALANCE SHEET RESULTS

Firm 1's balance sheets at the country/market and consolidated levels portray a company that is financially secure and is poised for a strong performance in the future. Its major strength lies in its large reserve of retained earnings and its lack of debt in any form. MagnaArgus is also very liquid, as it has a large hoard of cash and its inventory of sub-assemblies will turn into television sets in the next quarter. Accounts receivables in the total amount of $3,698,633 will also be collected in Quarter 1, 2004.

CASH FLOW OPERATIONS

Cash flow operations for your company in *The Global Business Game* can become somewhat complicated because of the large number of transactions involved. The cash inflow and outflow work sheets supplied in Appendix B may help you in this regard. After working with them for a while, many teams create spreadsheet versions to eliminate much of the quarterly, repetitive mathematics involved. For your interest a completed spreadsheet-based cash flow analysis of MagnaArgus' Quarter 4, 2003 operation can be found at *The Global Business Game*'s Web site in a file labeled "Chapter5CashFlow." The address of this website is: http://www.swcollege.com/management/gbg/gbg.html.

To help you better understand your company's cash flow operations, Exhibit 5.11 itemizes the firm's cash flow operation for the United States using one of the cash flow forms found in Appendix B, while Exhibits 5.12 (page 72) and 5.13 (page 73) explain how each of the values found in the cash flow model were obtained. As a test of your own understanding of the processes and accounts involved, you might try your hand at completing the form for its German and Japanese country units. After doing that, you can check your results against those presented at the game's Web site. By visiting the Web site you will also be able to review the various formulas embedded in the spreadsheet's many cells as well as the database needed to construct a viable cash flow model.

As seen in Exhibit 5.11, a total cash inflow, or surplus of US$44,548,167, was associated with Firm 1's American results. Its cash outflows were $14,694,544 while its inflows were $59,242,710, due mainly to carrying over a large cash account.

Exhibit 5.11   Sample Cash Flow Analysis, Quarter 4, 2003

CASH INFLOW	U.S.	Germany	Japan
Sales	9,269,580		
Cash Account	47,672,205		
Accounts Receivable	2,222,420		
Short-Term Investments	0		
Short-Term Loan	0		
Bond Sales	0		
Stock Sales	0		
Patents	0		
Subcontracting	0		
Capital Sales	0		
Liquidation/Salvaging	0		
Miscellaneous Credits	0		
Cash Transfers-In	78,505		
Total Cash In	59,242,710		

CASH OUTFLOW	U.S.	Germany	Japan
Factory Wages	2,156,507		
Subassemblies Purchases	2,284,845		
Advertising	13,000		
General Administration	187,165		
Distribution Centers	355,640		
Wholesalers/Sales Offices	1,012,762		
Sales Force/Trainees	143,688		
Training and Development	13,000		
Inventory Charges	204,183		
Shipping	227,058		
Patent Fees	0		
Subcontracting Cost	0		
Research and Development	5,000		
Quality Control/Programs	13,000		
Maintenance	48,850		
Income Tax	1,493,243		
Accounts Payable	1,136,603		
Overdraft Payment	0		
Interest	0		
Dividend	4,200,000		
Bond Call/Treasury Stock	0		
Capital In Progress	0		
Cash Transfers Out	1,200,000		
Total Cash Out	14,694,544		
Cash Surplus/Deficit	44,548,167		

ENTERING DECISIONS

The Player's Manual has now taken you through the mechanics of *The Global Business Game,* as well as directing you to a number of experiential exercises at its Web site that have been designed to help you form a dynamic, flexible, and productive top management group. The next and final chapter will deal with inputting your decisions into the simulation, obtaining your quarterly results, answering commonly asked questions about the game, and responding to various citical incidents your game administrator may employ.

Exhibit 5.12   U.S. Cash Inflow Operations

Inflow Item	Amount	Explanation
Sales	9,269,580	This is 80.0 percent of the country unit's net revenues for the quarter. The remaining 20.0 percent became an accounts receivable and will be a cash inflow item next quarter.
Cash Account	47,672,205	The previous quarter's balance brought forward.
Accounts Receivable	2,222,420	The remaining part of the previous quarter's net sales collected this quarter.
Short-Term Investments	0	The firm did not make any short-term investments.
Short-Term Loan	0	The firm did not take out a short-term loan.
Bond Sales	0	No bonds were sold this quarter. If sales had been made, the total value of the bond sale should be entered as the underwriting fees and first-quarter interest payment are treated later as cash outflows.
Stock Sale	0	No new shares of stock were sold this quarter. If stock had been sold, the issue's net proceeds should be entered.
Patents	0	The firm has not received any patents and has accordingly not been able to sell or license its patent to other firms in the industry.
Subcontracting	0	The company has not contracted out any of its capacity for manufacturing television sets to others in the industry.
Capital Sales	0	No sales or transfers of the unit's base capacity or automatons were completed this quarter. If a capital sale is made to another company in the industry, the sale's cash proceeds are entered. If the unit transfers any of its plant and equipment to another one of its country units, the asset's book value is treated as cash.
Liquidation	0	The firm did not liquidate its plant and equipment and therefore no cash values were obtained.
Salvaging	0	Upon a factory liquidation or decommissioning subassemblies are automatically salvaged at 30.0 percent of their market value. This amount would be treated as cash income.
Miscellaneous Credits	0	The game administrator did not levy any compensatory credits to the firm.
Cash Transfers In	78,505	Japan transferred ¥10,000,000 to the United States during the quarter. This amount was a cash outflow for the Japanese country unit and translated to $78,505 at the quarter's current exchange rate.

Exhibit 5.13   U.S. Cash Outflow Operations

Outflow Item	Amount	Explanation
Factory Wages	2,156,507	This is 90.0 percent of the wage bill generated by the number of line workers on payroll. The remaining 10.0 percent is an accounts payable. Note that the factory's wage bill may not be the firm's cost of goods sold.
Subassemblies Purchases	2,284,845	Seventy-five percent of the market value of new subassemblies purchased for next quarter's factory operations.
Advertising	13,000	A current cash expense as budgeted.
General Administration	187,165	Seventy percent of the country unit's current general administration expenses. The residual value becomes an accounts payable due the following quarter.
Distribution Centers	355,640	This amount includes the cost of performing warranty work.
Wholesalers/Sales Offices	1,012,762	This amount includes the factory's sales office.
Sales Force/Trainees	143,688	Seventy percent of the base salaries and commissions paid to all sales representatives on payroll at the end of the quarter. Budgeted sales force training and development funds are placed in this account.
Training and Development	13,000	Budgeted training funds expended on line workers and automaton technicians.
Inventory Charges	204,183	The cost of handling and storing all finished goods and subassemblies held on the country unit's books.
Shipping	227,058	All shipping charges associated with the purchase of subassemblies and the incoming transfer of finished goods from other firms or the firm's own country units.
Patent Fees	0	The company did not purchase any patent licenses from other firms.
Subcontracting Cost	0	The firm did not purchase television sets from other firms in the industry for resale under the firm's own brand name.
Research and Development	5,000	As budgeted for the quarter.
Quality Control/Programs	13,000	The firm's budgeted quality control programs and any quality inspection programs. All units destroyed through destructive testing are considered a noncash expense but a cost to the Quality Control Department.
Maintenance	48,850	As budgeted.
Income Tax	1,493,243	A cash outflow when positive and zero when negative.
Accounts Payable	1,136,603	A flexible account that varies somewhat with the firm's liquidity. When the firm is very liquid, all accounts payable are processed. When the firm approaches a liquidity problem, some payments to vendors are delayed.
Overdraft Payment	0	The firm had no emergency loans. This payment is automatically deducted from the quarter's cash flow and should be anticipated by the company.
Interest	0	The interest on any short-term loans and bonds.
Dividend	4,200,000	The firm declared a 0.50 cent per/share dividend on 8,400,000 shares of outstanding stock. This value was deducted from the company's cash account and retained earnings.
Bond Call/Treasury Stock	0	The firm does not have any bonds outstanding.
Capital In Progress	0	No new capital or land for a factory was purchased by the firm. The value here includes only the cost of the capital itself and not the supervisory charge demanded by the installation of any plant and equipment.
Cash Transfers Out	1,200,000	The company sent $1,200,000 to its German operations. This was a cash inflow to the Germany country unit amounting to €1,120,080.

Chapter 6

Simulation Operations and Playing Procedures

We have now come to the part of the game where you must transfer all your company's decisions to a form that can be used by your game administrator and the simulation itself. You will basically be interacting with the game using a 3.5-inch floppy company disk or files, although you will be installing the game's program's on your personal computer from the CD found in this manual. After every company in your industry has submitted their decisions, your game administrator will process them and you will receive feedback on your company's performance. These results will be handed back to you via your company disk or a similar file.

This chapter deals with how your game will be typically configured at most locations. There are a number of options your game administrator can employ for interacting with the game's model, such as a Web site, faxes between you and all parties connected with the industry being simulated, or a local area network (LAN). Your game administrator will explain the procedures in effect at your institution.

GENERAL DISKETTE OPERATIONS AND PROCEDURES

You have a CD in this Player's Manual that contains GBGPlayer. This application is needed to run your part of the simulation. Your team will have to supply its own 1.44MB floppy disk which you should prominently identify as being from your company. This disk is used to enter your firm's quarterly decisions and to retrieve your results each quarter. To interact with the programs, you must first install the CD's program on the computer you are using. Once that application has been installed, you can then enter and later access the results from the game. It is possible that the distribution CD found in this manual will have to be updated to keep GBGPlayer current. All updates can be found under "Player Resources" at the game's Web site at http://www.swcollege.com/management/gbg/gbg.html.

The initial installation of GBGPlayer, your company initialization process, and the game's quarterly decision set input and output steps follows the process diagrammed in Exhibit 6.1 (page 75). If you have a dedicated laptop or desktop computer, you will only have to install GBGPlayer once. If you do not have a dedicated personal computer, or are perhaps installing and using GBGPlayer on a shared computer in your school or business's computer laboratory, the GBG's program will probably be automatically removed from the system after its use. In this case, you will have to reinstall GBGPlayer each time it is used. If that is your situation, the sequence, after initializing your firm, would follow the path with the dotted line each time you enter your firm's decision set.

SYSTEM REQUIREMENTS

To run GBGPlayer you will need a personal computer with the following configuration and memory sizes:

Computer/Processor	Personal or multimedia computer with an 80486 or higher processor.
Operating System	Microsoft Windows® 95, Windows® 98, Windows® Millennia, Windows® 2000, Windows® NT 4.0, or Windows® XP.
Memory	In Windows® 95 or 98, 8MB of RAM.
	In Windows® Millennia, 2000, NT and XP, 16MB of RAM.

Disk Drives:
    Hard Disk   12MB of free hard-drive space
    CD-ROM   A standard CD-ROM drive.
    Floppy   1.44MB
Monitor   VGA or higher-resolution video adapter. Super VGA, 256-color ideal.
Peripherals   Any printer supported by Windows®.
                           Windows®-compatible mouse or other pointing device.

USING WINDOWS®

The Global Business Game assumes you have a working familiarity with Windows®, its screen layouts, and its operating conventions. If this is not the case, you may wish to refer to any of the following books for the rudiments required.

Crawford, S., & N. Salkind. (1998). *The ABCs of Windows® 98*. Alameda, CA: Sybex International.
Matthews, M. (1998). *Microsoft Windows® 98 companion*. Redmond, WA: Microsoft Press.
Rathbone, A. (1998). *Windows® 98 for dummies*. Foster City, CA: IDG Books International.
Stinson, C. (1998). *Running Microsoft Windows® 98*. Redmond, WA: Microsoft Press.

PLAYER APPLICATION INSTALLATION

Do the following to install *The Global Business Game* on your computer:

1. After opening Windows®, insert the **GBG Program** CD in your computer's CD tray. This will normally be your "D" drive.
2. Left-click on **Browse.** Select the **D drive** and then double-left-click on **Setup.exe.**
3. Follow the installation wizard instructions that appear on the screen.

After you have completed the installation process, you can launch **GBGPlayer** by either (1) choosing **Start/ Programs/The Global Business Game** and then **GBGPlayer,** or by (2) double-left-clicking on the GBGPlayer icon that was placed on your desktop when GBGPlayer was installed on your computer.

Exhibit 6.1   Using GBGPlayer

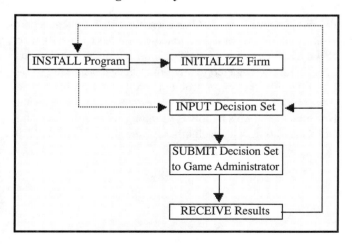

COMPANY INITIALIZATION

Before you can begin inputting your company's first round of decisions, you must first identify your company, the industry in which it is competing, and the members of your management team. It is assumed at this point you have been assigned to a company and your game administrator has provided you with the industry letter that applies to your company. These letters can run from "A" to "I". When you are in Windows®, launch *The Global Business Game* by choosing **Start/Programs/The Global Business Game,** and then **GBG Player,** or by double-clicking on GBGPlayer's icon on your desktop.

You will first see a screen that identifies *The Global Business Game,* followed shortly by a **Getting Started** screen. Because you are a new management team, click on "Initialize Your Company." This will be followed by a screen that asks you to identify your company with its name and the password you will be using to protect your files after the game has begun.

Complete the information required in the **Company Identification** window that appears. Create a name for your company, then insert your industry letter and firm number along with a password of your own choosing. Your decision disk is passworded so your competitors cannot intercept it and use its contents for their own purposes. Be sure to write down your password and ensure that all members of your management team know the password. If you forget your password, it cannot be retrieved—even by your game administrator. In such cases you will have to reinitialize your company after obtaining an updated and newly passworded disk from your game administrator.

The next part of the initializing process asks your company to list the names, telephone numbers, e-mail addresses, and student identification numbers of all those in your management group. See Screen 6.2 (page 78). You are providing this information so your game administrator can contact members of your firm should any problems occur with your decision input.

The final part of initializing your company requires you to save this input (Screen 6.3, page 78). You will probably be asked by your game administrator to choose "Save Firm to a Diskette," as your decision disk will be the one used to input your decisions to the game's main program. If your game administrator wants you to save your decision set to a file, a new "Save As" drop-down menu will appear that will display the location that has been designated for your decision set. Click on "Save," which will save your decision set under the label shown in the "File Name" box. Do not change the name of this file, as it is the only one that can be recognized by the simulation's main program.

At this point you have initialized your firm and have created a disk that is usable for your game administrator. Before logging off your computer, it would be a good idea to save your decision set diskette to (1) a backup floppy if you do not have a dedicated personal computer or (2) the hard drive of your personal computer if it is under your control.

CREATING AN EFFECTIVE MANAGEMENT TEAM

Many teams playing *The Global Business Game* are initially overwhelmed by what has been presented to them. Their natural inclination is to dive in and see what develops. The most vociferous or assertive team member can easily take the firm down the wrong path, as this person seems to know the way out of the jungle of information and challenges facing the group and the rest of the team follows. Remember that those engaged in any group decision-making exercise or situation, however, must solve two issues if it is to be effective: the *social* problem and the *task* problem. The social problem deals with work group relations, including peer relations, social hierarchy, leadership roles, and what is acceptable and unacceptable behavior. It basically involves how the group's members get along with each other, and embraces those small social matters that make people want to spend time with each other for the sheer fun of it.

Screen 6.1   Starting GBGPlayer and Initializing Your Company

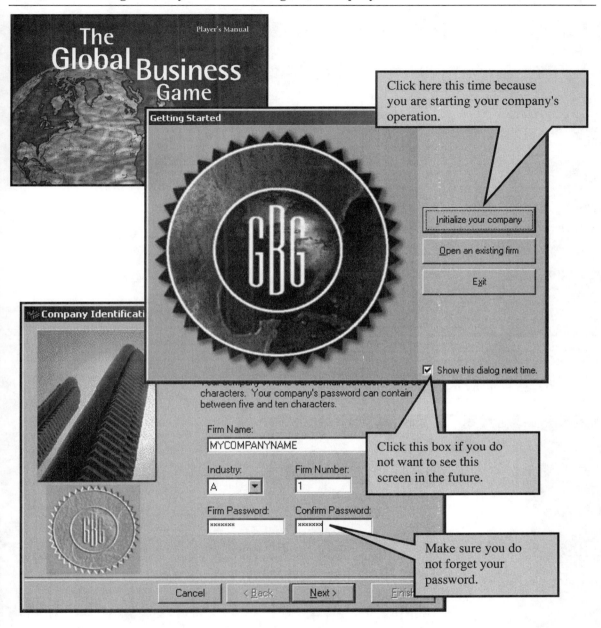

The other problem is the group's task problem. This involves understanding the concepts and skills required to facilitate an understanding of the group's tasks while assembling or developing the skills and ideas necessary for accomplishing results. Some decision-making teams emphasize the tasks confronting them, but neglect to service the group's social needs. Sometimes they just hope the social aspects do not get in their way. Other decision-making groups have a great time being together, but often sacrifice optimal economic or task performance results for social performance or their own sense of personal well-being.

Screen 6.2   Company Roster

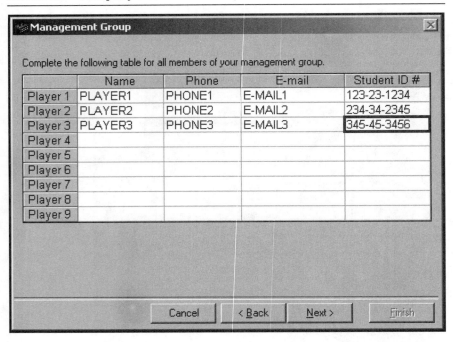

Screen 6.3   Saving Company Input

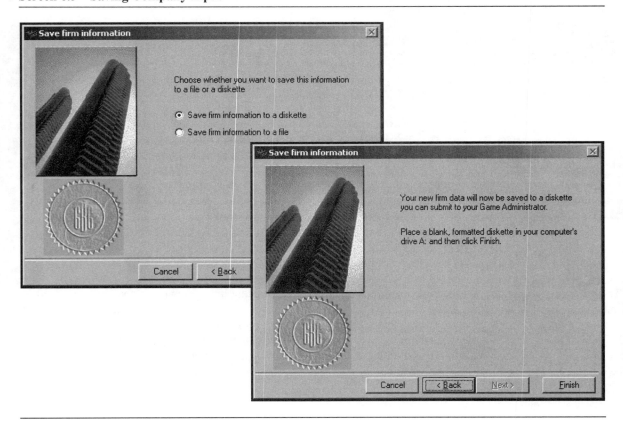

Because both potential problems must be addressed if you are going to have a socially stable and economically effective management team in *The Global Business Game,* your group will find it worthwhile to engage in the social and task-oriented exercises found at the game's Web site at http://www.swcollege.com/management/gbg/gbg.html. These exercises, or others that your instructor may have you perform, are useful for both game-playing and real-world executive decision-making groups. Take the time now to go "through the ropes" before the game begins and you'll start off on a stronger footing regarding the goals and objectives possessed by each member of your team. You will also gain a better understanding of the goals and objectives your company has decided to pursue, using your time together efficiently and also satisfying your own learning needs.

FORMAL DECISION RECORDS

The more successful firms in both business games and the real world are "planful" and orderly in their decision-making processes. A number of quarterly decision logs can be found in Appendix A. The entries in these logs summarize, and neatly tie together, the disparate decisions you have made by country market for each of your firm's functional areas. As you go through your group's decision-making process, enter your decisions in pencil (you will be changing entries many times before you decide on the final ones) in the current quarter's log. At the end of your decision-making session, you should review *as a group* all the entries you have made in your log to ensure they are the ones you really want to have implemented.

ENTERING AND EDITING COMPANY DECISIONS

The GBG has been designed to look and feel like a typical Windows® application. It has an opening sequence and a main tool bar. Through the use of this tool bar you can open as many windows as you like. And, as in Windows®, these windows can be maximized, minimized, dragged, or reshaped.

To enter GBGPlayer, launch the application in the normal fashion. This time, however, because your company has already been initialized you will be opening a new file for your now-existing firm. Click on **File** and then **Open.** "Open File" appears as in Screen 6.4 (page 80). It is assumed here you are using your 3.5-inch 1.44MB floppy in Drive A. Use the "Look in" combination box to get to your floppy, which is now in Drive A. Click on "Open" after highlighting the "3 1/2 Floppy (A:)" icon within the desktop layout map displayed.

Your firm's identification file will appear along with other files associated with the game. In the example shown, the identification file is "A_MagnaArgus Corporation.gbg", which was the name chosen for the company and industry example in Chapter 2. This is *Not* the file you want. You want instead the file that is associated with the current quarter's decision period. In this case, it is the file labeled "IndustryA1-MagnaArgus Corporation-Q1 2003.gbg" because we will be using this firm's decision set to explain the game's data-entry procedures. Double-click or highlight the correct file and click "Open". You will then be asked to pass a security check. You have three chances here before striking out.

After passing the security check, Screen 6.5 (on apge 81) appears. This is the first of six regular decision "pages" you will use to enter your decisions each quarter. The A column itemizes the decisions that must be made within the game's functional area. The B column, with its numbers in blue, reminds you of the decisions your company made last quarter. The C column asks you to update or revise each of the decisions that are needed in the current quarter. Tabs at the bottom of the screen let you page through the game's marketing, logistics, subassembly, production, plant, and finance decision areas while the screen's spin box allows you to dial the country unit for which you are making decisions.

This window also presents GBGPlayers' tool bar. It has six tools: **File, Edit, Decision Set, Reports, Windows,** and **Help.** You may be familiar with some of these tools such as **File, Edit, Windows,** and **Help.** Others, or their contents, are unique to *The Global Business Game.* The GBGPlayer tool **File** allows you to enter "New", which is used for creating a new company, or "Open", which is used to open your firm's files after you have initialized your company. It is here that you "Save" your decision and "Print" your results after your diskette has been returned to you by the game administrator. **Edit** gives you the opportunity to cut, paste, and copy entries. The **Windows** menu selection

Screen 6.4   Opening Firm Files

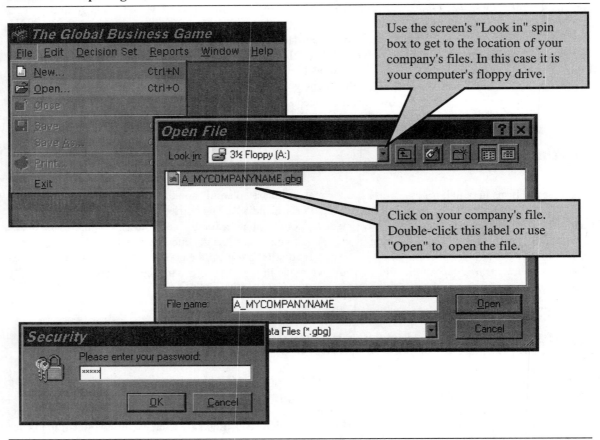

Use the screen's "Look in" spin box to get to the location of your company's files. In this case it is your computer's floppy drive.

Click on your company's file. Double-click this label or use "Open" to open the file.

allows you to arrange any screens you may have open simultaneously. **Help** allows you to search the game's key topics. **Reports** and **Decision Set** are unique tool bar items. The drop-down menu associated with **Reports** gives you access to the simulation's industry report, your company report, market research reports provided by the Merlin Group, and industry-wide bulletins. **Decision Set** receives the decisions you have made for the quarter and year in play.

DECISION ENTRIES

You will spend the greatest amount of your time in the application's **Decision Set** section. Screens 6.6–6.9 (pages 82–85) show you the decisions Firm 1, the MagnaArgus Corporation, will implement in January 2003, along with comments on those decisions. This has been done to indicate the nature of the entries your company must make every quarter. The decisions shown are for illustrative purposes only and are not necessarily optimal. By their inclusion it is also not suggested these are the decision areas your firm should address in the game's early rounds.

OCCASIONAL EVENTS

Over the game's run you may wish to take special, occasional actions, or may have to respond to critical incidents invoked by your game administrator. These actions can entail asset sales to other firms in your industry of either sub-

Screen 6.5   Tools and Tabs

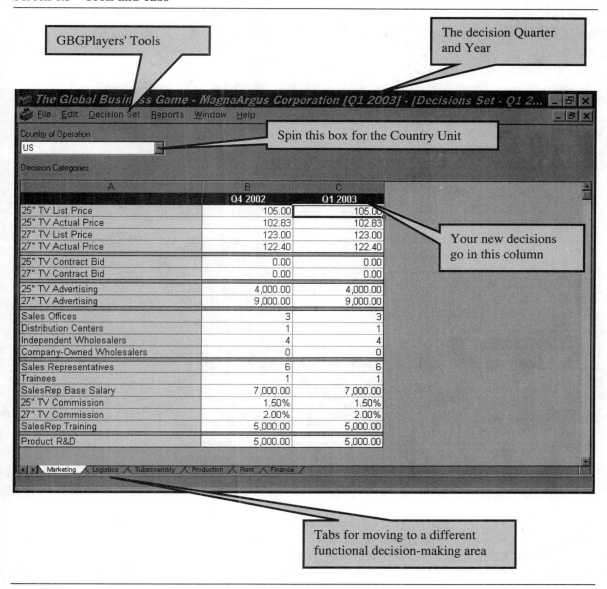

GBGPlayers' Tools

The decision Quarter and Year

The Global Business Game - MagnaArgus Corporation [Q1 2003] - [Decisions Set - Q1 2...

File   Edit   Decision Set   Reports   Window   Help

Country of Operation

US

Spin this box for the Country Unit

Decision Categories

A	B	C
	Q4 2002	Q1 2003
25" TV List Price	105.00	105.00
25" TV Actual Price	102.83	102.83
27" TV List Price	123.00	123.00
27" TV Actual Price	122.40	122.40
25" TV Contract Bid	0.00	0.00
27" TV Contract Bid	0.00	0.00
25" TV Advertising	4,000.00	4,000.00
27" TV Advertising	9,000.00	9,000.00
Sales Offices	3	3
Distribution Centers	1	1
Independent Wholesalers	4	4
Company-Owned Wholesalers	0	0
Sales Representatives	6	6
Trainees	1	1
SalesRep Base Salary	7,000.00	7,000.00
25" TV Commission	1.50%	1.50%
27" TV Commission	2.00%	2.00%
SalesRep Training	5,000.00	5,000.00
Product R&D	5,000.00	5,000.00

Your new decisions go in this column

Marketing   Logistics   Subassembly   Production   Plant   Finance

Tabs for moving to a different functional decision-making area

contracted television sets, patents, or automatons, and intrafirm automaton transfers between any of your country units. These actions are accomplished by various methods in the game.

Intrafirm automaton transfers are a unilateral action you can take at any time. To accomplish a transfer, access "Asset Transfers" within "Decision Set" (Screen 6.10, page 86). As presented in Screen 6.11 (page 87), the menu reminds you of the automatons and base capacity you have available for transfer by country unit and the various countries that can receive them. Recall from Chapter 4 that you must have land and plant capacity already in existence in a country targeted for an asset transfer for the transfer to be successful. Those countries eligible for an asset transfer will be highlighted while the ineligible countries will remain grayed out on the "Asset Transfer" menu. You can engage in these activities without notifying your game administrator.

Over the simulation's run your game administrator may want to use some of the "Critical Incidents in Global Industries" found in Appendix E. These incidents bring a number of additional dimensions to the game and involve a number

Screen 6.6   Marketing Decisions

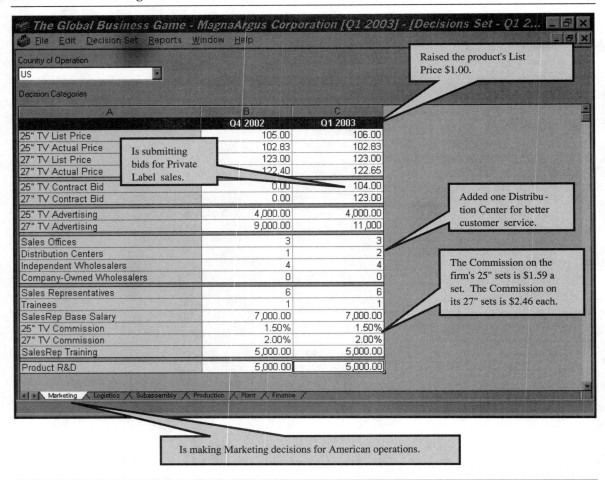

of the intangibles of managerial decision making. They can be invoked at any time by the game administrator. If a critical incident is in effect for a particular quarter, an appropriate announcement will be posted to the global industry report's bulletin board, as highlighted in Screen 6.12 (page 88).

Four responses are available to your company for each incident. Be sure you respond to each critical incident via the decision set portion of GBGPlayer's tool bar. If your firm does not respond, it will be automatically fined the equivalent of $50,000 for each missing response. This fine is processed through your home country's miscellaneous account.

The incidents themselves introduce you to a situation as a "mini case" that requires an immediate decision. In reviewing the choices available, you may feel that none are adequate, or, conversely, that each alternative possesses merit. Discuss among your management group the pros and cons of each alternative and choose the one you think is best based on your knowledge of both the critical incident's situation and an enlightened real-world response to the same issues posed by the incident. The choices you make for the incidents will directly and indirectly affect your firm's profitability. These effects will be strongest in the simulation's current decision-making quarter and will be completely dissipated within one year of the choice's occurrence.

Another occasional decision entails the purchase of any special Merlin Group studies. These are purchased via "Decision Set", "Merlin Group Report Requests". Screen 6.13 shows you the drop-down menu that allows you to make your purchases. As you check off the desired reports, their total cost is summed. This amount will appear as a home country miscellaneous expense. In this example, MagnaArgus is spending $4,000.00 to get data on Questions 1, 3, and 6.

Screen 6.7   Merchandise Logistics and Subassembly Decisions

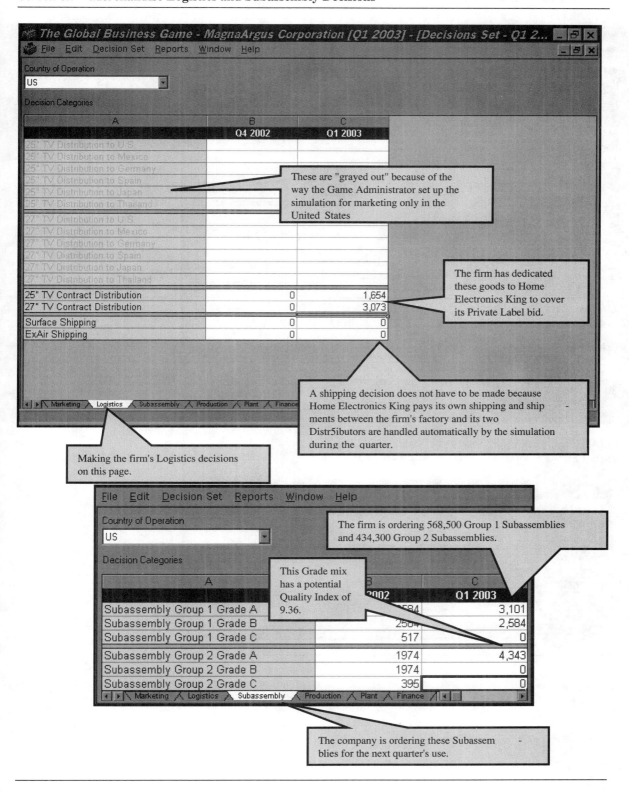

Screen 6.8   Plant Operations and Plant Capacity Decisions

Country of Operation

US

Decision Categories

A	B	C
	Q4 2002	Q1 2003
Shift 1 25" TV	23800	23800
Shift 2 25" TV	23800	23800
Shift 1 27" TV	00	46100
Shift 2 27" TV	00	46100
Line Supervisors	2	4
Shift 1 25" TV Workers	57	59
Shift 2 25" TV Workers	56	57
Shift 1 27" TV Workers		56
Shift 2 27" TV Workers	56	57
Automaton Technicians	3	3
Line Worker Training	0.00	4,000.00
Automaton Technician Training	4,000.00	4,000.00
Quality Control Training	13,000.00	13,000.00
Quality Control Sampling Program		

The company wants better control of its assembly line workers.

To have an average of 204 Line Workers each workday the firm is putting 229 workers on its factory payroll.

Marketing Logistics Subassembly **Production** Plant Finance

File   Edit   Decision Set   Reports   Window   Help

Country of Operation

US

Decision Categories

These new Automatons, when they go on-line in Q3 2003, will be able to make 5,777 25" sets or 5,200 27" TVs.

A	B	C
	Q4 2002	Q1 2003
New Base Capacity	0	0
New Automaton 1 Machines	0	5
New Automaton 2 Machines	0	0
Line Maintenance	4,500.00	4,500.00
Automaton 1 Maintenance	110.00	110.00
Automaton 2 Maintenance	250.00	250.00
☐ Decommission Plant		
☐ Liquidate Plant		

Marketing Logistics Subassembly Production **Plant** Finance

Screen 6.9: Finance Decisions

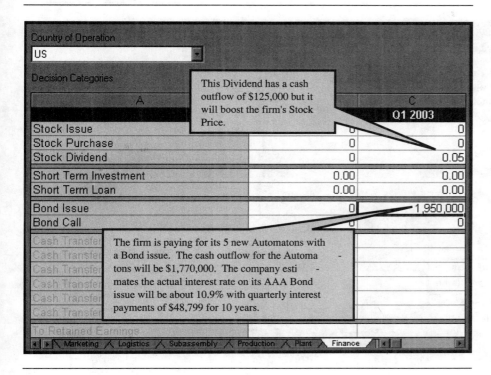

SAVING DECISION SETS

When you have completed your firm's set of decisions for the quarter, return to **File** and select **Save.** This action stores the work you have done thus far. If you use the command "Save As", your decision file or decision set for the quarter will be saved under a new name you assign to it and possibly to a different location of your choice. Under most circumstances you should not use "Save As" because it creates a file name that is not directly readable by the simulation.

As part of the game's data entry routine, GBGPlayer will perform a moderate editing of your decisions to make sure they are acceptable to the game's model. This editing will not fix or make incorrect decisions "correct." It merely edits them so they can be processed by the game's programs. If any of your company's decisions cannot be accepted by the game (and these are usually typographical errors, number transpositions, or data in the wrong spreadsheet fields), the simulation will "hang up" during processing and your game administrator will have to contact you to obtain an acceptable entry from your group.

After reviewing your firm's decision inputs, it is a good idea to print out your decision set for your records and to make sure the decisions you entered on your decision disk are the same ones you had on your decision logs. This is done by clicking on **File** and then on **Print.** Once you have submitted your decision set, it is very difficult to correct any decision or data input mistakes you have made.

VIEWING AND PRINTING RESULTS

After you have submitted your decision set to the game administrator, your firm's results will be returned to you via the same decision disk. To get your results under Windows®, launch *The Global Business Game*. Go through the same security clearance after clicking on "Open" and accessing your company's file found on your floppy. Click on **Reports.** A drop-down menu will appear and you can choose the particular report you would like to view. You can either print out your results from the screen or by going to **Print** within the **File** menu or CTRL F within the screen you are viewing.

Screen 6.10: Interfirm Asset Transfers

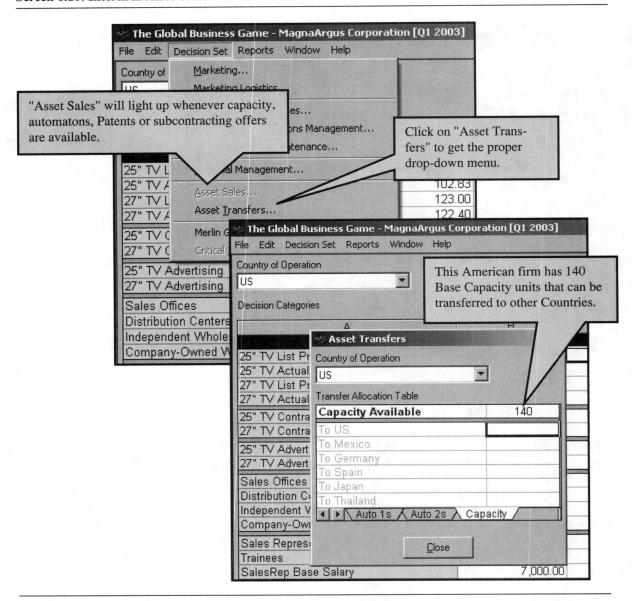

TROUBLESHOOTING AND COMMONLY ASKED QUESTIONS

Most questions players have about business game they are playing center around "Why did this happen?" or "I don't understand how the game does this!" Every question you may have about the game as, in life, cannot be explained fully. What *can* be answered, however, are various items you may have overlooked or have not even considered when making a decision. In doing this you may have caused the unanticipated or unexplainable results you and your company have obtained. Exhibit 6.2 (page 89) lists various questions and suggested answers by the game's major functional areas of marketing, production, finance, and accounting.

Screen 6.11: Responding to Critical Incidents

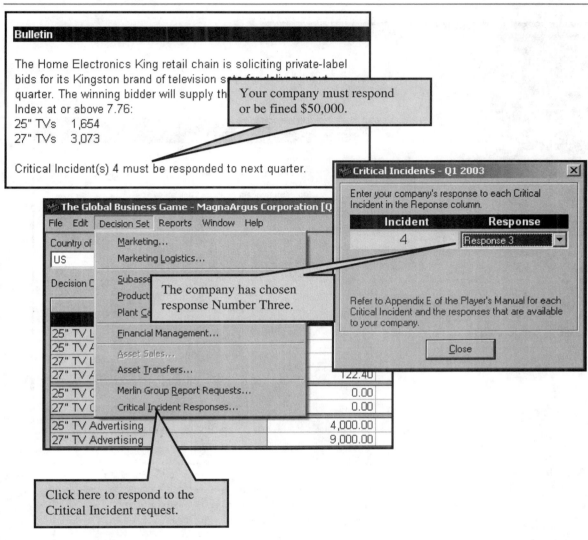

GETTING HELP

While this chapter's previous section dealt with commonly asked questions about how to work with certain aspects of your company, you can get additional help at any time when you are operating within *The Global Business Game*. This is done by going to **Help** on the game's tool bar. This **Help** routine operates in the same fashion as that found in any Windows® application. **Help** covers all the game manual's contents and procedures, provides quick definitions for all entries appearing on the game's printouts, and has an index for searching various topics within **Help**. If you are unfamiliar with how **Help** operates, or how to be efficient with its use, you can click on "How to use Help" within the **Help** menu.

Screen 6.12   Requesting Merlin Group Reports

The Global Business Game - MagnaArgus Corporation [Q1 2003]

File   Edit   Decision Set   Reports   Window   Help

Country of
US

Decision

Marketing...
Marketing Logistics...
Subassembly Purchases...
Production & Operations Management...
Plant Capacity & Maintenance...
Financial Management...
Asset Sales...
Asset Transfers...
Merlin Group Report Requests...
Critical Incident Responses...

25" TV L
25" TV A
27" TV L
27" TV A
25" TV C
27" TV C
25" TV Advertising
27" TV Advertising

Click here under Decision Sets to
order Merlin Group Studies.

Merlin Group Report Requests - Q1 2003

Question #	Information Provided	Charge	Purchase
1	All company 25" TV unit sales by country.	$1,500.00	☑
2	All company 27" set unit sales by country.	$1,500.00	☐
3	Near-term forecast of 25" set unit sales by country.	$500.00	☑
4	Near-term forecast of 27" set unit sales by country.	$500.00	☐
5	Near-term forecast of unit demand for 25" and 27" private label sets.	$1,000.00	☐
6	All company 25" set Quality Indices by country.	$2,000.00	☑
7	All company 27" set Quality Indices by country.	$2,000.00	☐
8	Sales Representative Compensation by company and country	$750.00	☐
9	All company 25" set Advertising budgets by country.	$250.00	☐
10	All company 27" set Advertising budgets by country.	$250.00	☐
11	Estimated R&D budgets by company and country.	$300.00	☐
12	Estimated QC budgets by company and country.	$300.00	☐
	Totals	$4,000.00	3

Close

Three special studies have been requested costing
$4,000.00. This amount will be processed through
the firm's Miscellaneous account.

DECISION-MAKING AIDS

In the name of efficiency and orderliness, the more effective firms in a business game quickly go about creating deci-sion-making aids for themselves. Much of what is in *The Global Business Game* is routine or tactical, just like in the real world. Other parts are "soft" and require occasional strategic decisions. You should separate the two so that your creative powers can be focused on the areas that can be solved only through study and intuition.

Your manual contains a number of forms that help you through the planning and evaluation process your team should go through each quarter. The appendixes contain forms for creating *pro forma* income statements, balance sheets, and cash flow projections. These forms can easily be converted into spreadsheet models that can be shared with your partners and it would be wise for you to do so. The game's Web site at http://www.swcollege.com/management/gbg/gbg.html under "Game Administrator Resources" also contains examples of the types of spreadsheet decision-making aids players have found useful. Your game administrator may make these available to your company or may

Exhibit 6.2   Frequently Asked Questions

Marketing

"I haven't been able to get a patented feature for my TVs, even although I've spent a lot of R&D money on the effort."	The simulation rewards a constant stream of R&D money, so you may have been spending irregular amounts over the past number of quarters. Also, what you think is "a lot of money" may not be very much. You can find out the R&D budgets of various firms in your industry by buying a market research study from the Merlin Group. This would indicate to you what your competitors are doing and if they are perhaps having the same experience that you are having.
"I'd like to trick my competitors by posting a very high list price for my TVs while actually selling them for a very low actual price. Do you think this is a good idea?"	In doing this you may fool somebody for a while, but your firm's actual prices are divulged to your competitors the following quarter. In doing this you are also costing your firm money, as sales representative commissions are paid on your list prices, although you are collecting revenue only on your actual prices.
"I think our company has enough quality to really get high sales. How do I let my customers know I have high quality?"	The best you can do here is to engage in more total sales promotion efforts than your competitors. Make sure your advertising budgets, sales representative base salaries, and unit commissions are higher, on a per unit basis, than those of your competition. It would also be wise to get a market research study from the Merlin Group to check whether the quality ratings on your TVs are really that much better than your competition's. You may be trying to advertise something you actually do not have.
"Can I design "better" advertisements than those being used by my rivals?"	No, you cannot design better advertisements, but you can out-advertise your competitors by spending more money than they do.

Production

"No matter how I figure it, my unit costs are always different than what I forecast."	After things settle down in your plant, you should be able to calculate your unit costs fairly accurately. Some of the reasons why you may be off when forecasting unit costs are associated with down time caused by running out of subassemblies or worker absenteeism during the quarter, not correctly calculating the weighted cost of the mix of subassembly grades used in the production run, and the higher wage rates forced on 25-inch TVs when you have them assembled by 27-inch line workers.
"The number of labor hours delivered by my workers never comes up to what I have ordered. What causes this?"	The number of workers who actually come to work each day, week, and quarter is related to your firm's maintenance budget at each plant and the number of vacation days, sick days, and absenteeism rates associated with each country's labor practices and work ethic. You can affect the non-delivery of labor hours by increasing your maintenance budgets. You cannot affect those factors tied to each country's labor practices and work ethic. In this area you must anticipate these realities, which are presented in Exhibit 5.7 in your Player's Manual.
"I'm getting a lot of returns and high warranty charges. How can I get rid of them?"	Returns cannot be completely eliminated, but you can minimize them by producing TVs with greater intrinsic quality and/or increasing the level of the quality control inspections programs at each factory. You can produce sets with greater intrinsic quality by increasing the number of line supervisors you have per shift, engaging in more work crew training programs, and using more automatons as part of your assembly operations.

Continued

Exhibit 6.2   Frequently Asked Questions *(Continued)*

Production

"How do I know if my maintenance budgets are either too high or too low?"	You can determine if your maintenance budgets are correct by looking at your operations report's maintenance effect statistic. If it is over an index value of 1.00, the overall budget is too high; if it is below 1.00, it is too low. Because this index value is for your total budget, you still may not know which maintenance component is incorrect, as these components are spread over the plant and its assembly line mechanics and two types of automatons. The best indication that these budgets are too low is when the number of labor hours available in your plant(s) falls. This decrease in actual labor hours indicates that some of your equipment was unusable due to poor maintenance and that you should increase this budget so that your assembly line does not experience downtime in future quarters.

Finance/Accounting

"How can I 'beef up' my firm's stock price?"	Your company's stock price is largely determined by your firm's earnings, its retained earnings, and the number of shares you have outstanding. You can "beef up" your firm's stock price by working on these three elements, that is, have high earnings, a large pool of retained earnings from which you can declare dividends, and relatively few shares outstanding. The latter element can be improved by purchasing Treasury stock, which reduces the number of shares outstanding, thereby increasing your firm's earnings-per-share.
"No matter how hard I try I always miscalculate my firm's cash flow needs! What is causing this?"	You are overlooking any one of the large number of items figured into your firm's cash flow needs. You may also not understand the leads and lags of the various flows associated with different operations. If you have all of the above correctly considered, the next major reason cash flows are not what they were projected to be is the fact that revenues, sales, and costs, mostly unit manufacturing costs, were more or less than forecasted. It may be that your sales projections were too high and therefore actual cash from sales was lower than anticipated. Perhaps your firm's unit manufacturing costs were greater than projected, therefore reducing the operating profit you had anticipated for the quarter.
"Why should I bother to plan a country unit's cash flow needs when the simulation automatically sends money to any unit that runs out of it during the quarter?"	It is true that the simulation will automatically "cover" a country unit's technical insolvency. Should this occur very often, however, it is possible your lack of financial planning may spread to your home country unit, which is actually the source of the funds that are being transferred to the insolvent country unit. When this occurs, the home country unit becomes insolvent and receives a very "sticky" C credit rating. This rating affects its cost of debt capital and also causes the corporation's stock price to fall.

require you to design you own as a useful exercise. It is believed it is better for your team to create its own spreadsheets. This is because by this method you will have created something that is personal, whose design is based on your own needs and perceptions. More important, if you can program your spreadsheets correctly, you will have obtained a real handle on at least the game's mechanics. This "handle" then frees your time so you can concentrate on the correctness of your firm's strategy and keeping all things on target.

Exhibit 6.3   A Bubble Chart Example

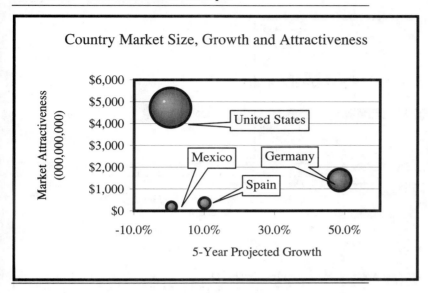

CHARTS AND GRAPHS

As part of the gaming experience, your game administrator or instructor may ask you to create reports or make formal in-class presentations. A number of very attractive charts can be easily constructed by your management team because *The Global Business Game* works within the Windows® operating system, which features cut, copy, and paste. The following section indicates some of the many charts and graphs that can be created using the tools available within GBGPlayer and Windows®.

Bubble Charts. The chart shown in Exhibit 6.3 is a customized version of that found in Exhibit 1.7 of your Player's Manual. In this case the game administrator has chosen an economic scenario where there is little growth in the NAFTA countries of Mexico and the United States, and moderate to high growth in the EU's Spain and Germany. Based on this presentation, a company wanting to emphasize revenues would put its efforts into the United States and Germany. If the firm wanted to emphasize growth, it would eliminate any current and projected lost sales and back orders while dedicating new resources to Spain and Germany. The chart itself was created by (1) obtaining from the game administrator the game's GDP levels, (2) copying and pasting the GDP data into an Excel spreadsheet, and then (3) using "Bubbles" from Excel's toolbar to create the final chart.

The Merlin Group's Clipboard. Although the Merlin Group studies your firm purchases are presented as format-ted reports within GBGPlayer, they are actually derived from Excel spreadsheets. You can transfer any report you have purchased to a spreadsheet program by clicking on the clipboard found in the report screen's lower-right-hand corner. In the example shown in Exhibit 6.4 (page 92), the firm has copied Question 10's output to the GBGPlayer clipboard, which was then pasted into an Excel worksheet. From the worksheet the company then used Excel's Bar Charts to present the information.

Exhibit 6.4   A Bar Chart Example

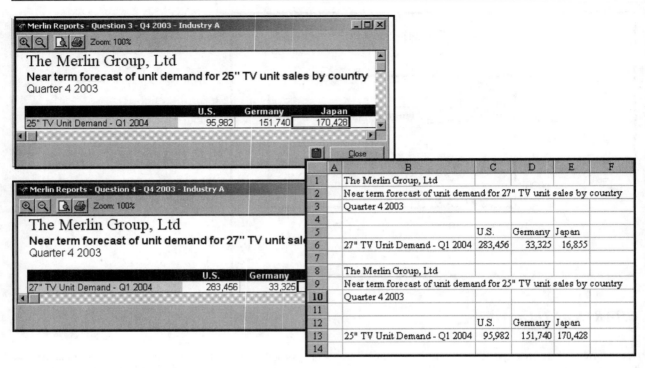

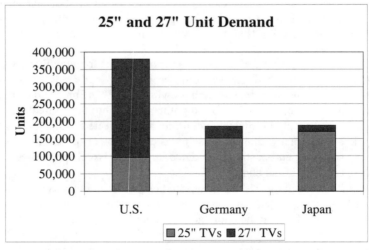

Appendixes

Appendix A: United States Decision Log

DECISION	4/2002	1/2003	2/2003	3/2003	4/2003	1/2004	2/2004	3/2004	4/2004	1/2005	2/2005	3/2005	4/2005
Marketing													
25" TV List Price													
25" TV Actual Price													
27" TV List Price													
27" TV Actual Price													
25" TV Contract Bid													
27" TV Contract Bid													
25" TV Advertising													
27" TV Advertising													
Sales Offices													
Distribution Centers													
Independent Wholesalers													
Company Wholesalers													
Sales Representatives													
Trainees													
SalesRep Base Salary													
25" TV Commission													
27" TV Commission													
SalesRep Training													
Product R&D													

Logistics

25" TVs to Mexico														
25" TVs to Germany														
25" TVs to Spain														
25" TVs to Japan														
25" TVs to Thailand														
27" TVs to Mexico														
27" TVs to Germany														
27" TVs to Spain														
27" TVs to Japan														
27" TVs to Thailand														
25" TV Contracts														
27" TV Contracts														
Surface Shipping														
ExAir Shipping														
Subassemblies														
Group 1 Grade A														
Group 1 Grade B														
Group 1 Grade C														
Group 2 Grade A														
Group 2 Grade B														
Group 2 Grade C														

Continued

Appendix A: United States Decision Log (Coontinued)

DECISION	4/2002	1/2003	2/2003	3/2003	4/2003	1/2004	2/2004	3/2004	4/2004	1/2005	2/2005	3/2005	4/2005
Production													
Shift 1 25″ TVs													
Shift 2 25″ TVs													
Shift 1 27″ TVs													
Shift 2 27″ TVs													
Line Supervisors													
Shift 1 25″ TV Workers													
Shift 2 25″ TV Workers													
Shift 1 27″ TV Workers													
Shift 2 27″ TV Workers													
Automaton Technicians													
Line Worker Training													
Automaton Tech. Training													
Quality Control Training													
QC Sample Program													

Plant

New Base Capacity																					
New Auto1s																					
New Auto2s																					
Line Maintenance																					
Automaton 1 Maintenance																					
Automaton 2 Maintenance																					
Decommission/Liquidation																					

Finance

Stock Issue/Purchase																					
Stock Dividend																					
Short-Term Investment																					
Short-Term Loan																					
Bond Issue/Call																					
Cash Transfer to Mexico																					
Cash Transfer to Germany																					
Cash Transfer to Spain																					
Cash Transfer to Japan																					
Cash Transfer to Thailand																					
To Retained Earnings																					

Appendix A: Mexico Decision Log

DECISION	4/2002	1/2003	2/2003	3/2003	4/2003	1/2004	2/2004	3/2004	4/2004	1/2005	2/2005	3/2005	4/2005
Marketing													
25″ TV List Price													
25″ TV Actual Price													
27″ TV List Price													
27″ TV Actual Price													
25″ TV Contract Bid													
27″ TV Contract Bid													
25″ TV Advertising													
27″ TV Advertising													
Sales Offices													
Distribution Centers													
Independent Wholesalers													
Company Wholesalers													
Sales Representatives													
Trainees													
SalesRep Base Salary													
25″ TV Commission													
27″ TV Commission													
SalesRep Training													
Product R&D													

Logistics

25" TVs to United States														
25" TVs to Germany														
25" TVs to Spain														
25" TVs to Japan														
25" TVs to Thailand														
27" TVs to United States														
27" TVs to Germany														
27" TVs to Spain														
27" TVs to Japan														
27" TVs to Thailand														
25" TV Contracts														
27" TV Contracts														
Surface Shipping														
ExAir Shipping														
Subassemblies														
Group 1 Grade A														
Group 1 Grade B														
Group 1 Grade C														
Group 2 Grade A														
Group 2 Grade B														
Group 2 Grade C														

Continued

Appendix A: Mexico Decision Log (*Continued*)

DECISION	4/2002	1/2003	2/2003	3/2003	4/2003	1/2004	2/2004	3/2004	4/2004	1/2005	2/2005	3/2005	4/2005
Production													
Shift 1 25″ TVs													
Shift 2 25″ TVs													
Shift 1 27″ TVs													
Shift 2 27″ TVs													
Line Supervisors													
Shift 1 25″ TV Workers													
Shift 2 25″ TV Workers													
Shift 1 27″ TV Workers													
Shift 2 27″ TV Workers													
Automaton Technicians													
Line Worker Training													
Automaton Tech. Training													
Quality Control Training													
QC Sample Program													

Plant																
New Base Capacity																
New Auto1s																
New Auto2s																
Line Maintenance																
Automaton 1 Maintenance																
Automaton 2 Maintenance																
Decommission/Liquidation																
Finance																
Stock Issue/Purchase																
Stock Dividend																
Short-Term Investment																
Short-Term Loan																
Bond Issue/Call																
Cash Transfer to United States																
Cash Transfer to Germany																
Cash Transfer to Spain																
Cash Transfer to Japan																
Cash Transfer to Thailand																
To Retained Earnings																

Appendix A: Germany Decision Log

DECISION	4/2002	1/2003	2/2003	3/2003	4/2003	1/2004	2/2004	3/2004	4/2004	1/2005	2/2005	3/2005	4/2005
Marketing													
25″ TV List Price													
25″ TV Actual Price													
27″ TV List Price													
27″ TV Actual Price													
25″ TV Contract Bid													
27″ TV Contract Bid													
25″ TV Advertising													
27″ TV Advertising													
Sales Offices													
Distribution Centers													
Independent Wholesalers													
Company Wholesalers													
Sales Representatives													
Trainees													
SalesRep Base Salary													
25″ TV Commission													
27″ TV Commission													
SalesRep Training													
Product R&D													

Logistics

25" TVs to United States													
25" TVs to Mexico													
25" TVs to Spain													
25" TVs to Japan													
25" TVs to Thailand													
27" TVs to United States													
27" TVs to Mexico													
27" TVs to Spain													
27" TVs to Japan													
27" TVs to Thailand													
25" TV Contracts													
27" TV Contracts													
Surface Shipping													
ExAir Shipping													
Subassemblies													
Group 1 Grade A													
Group 1 Grade B													
Group 1 Grade C													
Group 2 Grade A													
Group 2 Grade B													
Group 2 Grade C													

Continued

Appendix A: Germany Decision Log (Continued)

DECISION	4/2002	1/2003	2/2003	3/2003	4/2003	1/2004	2/2004	3/2004	4/2004	1/2005	2/2005	3/2005	4/2005
Production													
Shift 1 25" TVs													
Shift 2 25" TVs													
Shift 1 27" TVs													
Shift 2 27" TVs													
Line Supervisors													
Shift 1 25" TV Workers													
Shift 2 25" TV Workers													
Shift 1 27" TV Workers													
Shift 2 27" TV Workers													
Automaton Technicians													
Line Worker Training													
Automaton Tech. Training													
Quality Control Training													
QC Sample Program													

Plant																					
New Base Capacity																					
New Auto1s																					
New Auto2s																					
Line Maintenance																					
Automaton 1 Maintenance																					
Automaton 2 Maintenance																					
Decommission/Liquidation																					
Finance																					
Stock Issue/Purchase																					
Stock Dividend																					
Short-Term Investment																					
Short-Term Loan																					
Bond Issue/Call																					
Cash Transfer to United States																					
Cash Transfer to Mexico																					
Cash Transfer to Spain																					
Cash Transfer to Japan																					
Cash Transfer to Thailand																					
To Retained Earnings																					

Appendix A: Spain Decision Log

DECISION	4/2002	1/2003	2/2003	3/2003	4/2003	1/2004	2/2004	3/2004	4/2004	1/2005	2/2005	3/2005	4/2005
Marketing													
25" TV List Price													
25" TV Actual Price													
27" TV List Price													
27" TV Actual Price													
25" TV Contract Bid													
27" TV Contract Bid													
25" TV Advertising													
27" TV Advertising													
Sales Offices													
Distribution Centers													
Independent Wholesalers													
Company Wholesalers													
Sales Representatives													
Trainees													
SalesRep Base Salary													
25" TV Commission													
27" TV Commission													
SalesRep Training													
Product R&D													

Logistics

25" TVs to United States																				
25" TVs to Mexico																				
25" TVs to Germany																				
25" TVs to Japan																				
25" TVs to Thailand																				
27" TVs to United States																				
27" TVs to Mexico																				
27" TVs to Germany																				
27" TVs to Japan																				
27" TVs to Thailand																				
25" TV Contracts																				
27" TV Contracts																				
Surface Shipping																				
ExAir Shipping																				

Subassemblies

Group 1 Grade A																				
Group 1 Grade B																				
Group 1 Grade C																				
Group 2 Grade A																				
Group 2 Grade B																				
Group 2 Grade C																				

Continued

Appendix A: Spain Decision Log (*Continued*)

DECISION	4/2002	1/2003	2/2003	3/2003	4/2003	1/2004	2/2004	3/2004	4/2004	1/2005	2/2005	3/2005	4/2005
Production													
Shift 1 25″ TVs													
Shift 2 25″ TVs													
Shift 1 27″ TVs													
Shift 2 27″ TVs													
Line Supervisors													
Shift 1 25″ TV Workers													
Shift 2 25″ TV Workers													
Shift 1 27″ TV Workers													
Shift 2 27″ TV Workers													
Automaton Technicians													
Line Worker Training													
Automaton Tech. Training													
Quality Control Training													
QC Sample Program													

Plant

New Base Capacity																
New Auto1s																
New Auto2s																
Line Maintenance																
Automaton 1 Maintenance																
Automaton 2 Maintenance																
Decommission/Liquidation																

Finance

Stock Issue/Purchase																
Stock Dividend																
Short-Term Investment																
Short-Term Loan																
Bond Issue/Call																
Cash Transfer to United States																
Cash Transfer to Mexico																
Cash Transfer to Germany																
Cash Transfer to Japan																
Cash Transfer to Thailand																
To Retained Earnings																

Appendix A: Japan Decision Log

DECISION	4/2002	1/2003	2/2003	3/2003	4/2003	1/2004	2/2004	3/2004	4/2004	1/2005	2/2005	3/2005	4/2005
Marketing													
25" TV List Price													
25" TV Actual Price													
27" TV List Price													
27" TV Actual Price													
25" TV Contract Bid													
27" TV Contract Bid													
25" TV Advertising													
27" TV Advertising													
Sales Offices													
Distribution Centers													
Independent Wholesalers													
Company Wholesalers													
Sales Representatives													
Trainees													
SalesRep Base Salary													
25" TV Commission													
27" TV Commission													
SalesRep Training													
Product R&D													

Logistics												
25" TVs to United States												
25" TVs to Mexico												
25" TVs to Germany												
25" TVs to Spain												
25" TVs to Thailand												
27" TVs to United States												
27" TVs to Mexico												
27" TVs to Germany												
27" TVs to Spain												
27" TVs to Thailand												
25" TV Contracts												
27" TV Contracts												
Surface Shipping												
ExAir Shipping												
Subassemblies												
Group 1 Grade A												
Group 1 Grade B												
Group 1 Grade C												
Group 2 Grade A												
Group 2 Grade B												
Group 2 Grade C												

Continued

Appendix A: Japan Decision Log (*Continued*)

DECISION	4/2002	1/2003	2/2003	3/2003	4/2003	1/2004	2/2004	3/2004	4/2004	1/2005	2/2005	3/2005	4/2005
Production													
Shift 1 25″ TVs													
Shift 2 25″ TVs													
Shift 1 27″ TVs													
Shift 2 27″ TVs													
Line Supervisors													
Shift 1 25″ TV Workers													
Shift 2 25″ TV Workers													
Shift 1 27″ TV Workers													
Shift 2 27″ TV Workers													
Automaton Technicians													
Line Worker Training													
Automaton Tech. Training													
Quality Control Training													
QC Sample Program													

Plant

New Base Capacity																
New Auto1s																
New Auto2s																
Line Maintenance																
Automaton 1 Maintenance																
Automaton 2 Maintenance																
Decommission/Liquidation																

Finance

Stock Issue/Purchase																
Stock Dividend																
Short-Term Investment																
Short-Term Loan																
Bond Issue/Call																
Cash Transfer to United States																
Cash Transfer to Mexico																
Cash Transfer to Germany																
Cash Transfer to Spain																
Cash Transfer to Thailand																
To Retained Earnings																

Appendix A: Thailand Decision Log

DECISION	4/2002	1/2003	2/2003	3/2003	4/2003	1/2004	2/2004	3/2004	4/2004	1/2005	2/2005	3/2005	4/2005
Marketing													
25" TV List Price													
25" TV Actual Price													
27" TV List Price													
27" TV Actual Price													
25" TV Contract Bid													
27" TV Contract Bid													
25" TV Advertising													
27" TV Advertising													
Sales Offices													
Distribution Centers													
Independent Wholesalers													
Company Wholesalers													
Sales Representatives													
Trainees													
SalesRep Base Salary													
25" TV Commission													
27" TV Commission													
SalesRep Training													
Product R&D													

Logistics

25″ TVs to United States																	
25″ TVs to Mexico																	
25″ TVs to Germany																	
25″ TVs to Spain																	
25″ TVs to Japan																	
27″ TVs to United States																	
27″ TVs to Mexico																	
27″ TVs to Germany																	
27″ TVs to Spain																	
27″ TVs to Japan																	
25″ TV Contracts																	
27″ TV Contracts																	
Surface Shipping																	
ExAir Shipping																	
Subassemblies																	
Group 1 Grade A																	
Group 1 Grade B																	
Group 1 Grade C																	
Group 2 Grade A																	
Group 2 Grade B																	
Group 2 Grade C																	

Continued

Appendix A: Thailand Decision Log (Continued)

DECISION	4/2002	1/2003	2/2003	3/2003	4/2003	1/2004	2/2004	3/2004	4/2004	1/2005	2/2005	3/2005	4/2005
Production													
Shift 1 25" TVs													
Shift 2 25" TVs													
Shift 1 27" TVs													
Shift 2 27" TVs													
Line Supervisors													
Shift 1 25" TV Workers													
Shift 2 25" TV Workers													
Shift 1 27" TV Workers													
Shift 2 27" TV Workers													
Automaton Technicians													
Line Worker Training													
Automaton Tech. Training													
Quality Control Training													
QC Sample Program													

Plant

New Base Capacity														
New Auto1s														
New Auto2s														
Line Maintenance														
Automaton 1 Maintenance														
Automaton 2 Maintenance														
Decommission/Liquidation														
Finance														
Stock Issue/Purchase														
Stock Dividend														
Short-Term Investment														
Short-Term Loan														
Bond Issue/Call														
Cash Transfer to United States														
Cash Transfer to Mexico														
Cash Transfer to Germany														
Cash Transfer to Spain														
Cash Transfer to Japan														
To Retained Earnings														

Appendix B: United States Cash Inflow Work Sheet

CASH INFLOW	4/2002	1/2003	2/2003	3/2003	4/2003	1/2004	2/2004	3/2004	4/2004	1/2005	2/2005	3/2005	4/2005
Sales													
Cash Account													
Accounts Receivable													
Short-Term Investments													
Short-Term Loan													
Bond Sales													
Stock Sale													
Patents													
Subcontracting													
Capital Sales													
Liquidation/Salvaging													
Miscellaneous Credits													
Cash Transfers In													
Total Cash In													

CASH OUTFLOW	4/2002	1/2003	2/2003	3/2003	4/2003	1/2004	2/2004	3/2004	4/2004	1/2005	2/2005	3/2005	4/2005
Factory Wages													
Subassemblies Purchases													
Advertising													
General Administration													

	Distribution Centers	Wholesalers/Sales Offices	Sales Force/Trainees	Training and Development	Inventory Charges	Shipping	Patent Fees	Subcontracting Cost	Research and Development	Quality Control/Programs	Maintenance	Income Tax	Accounts Payable	Overdraft Payment	Interest	Dividend	Bond Call/Treasury Stock	Capital In Progress	Cash Transfers Out	Total Cash out	Cash Surplus/Deficit

Appendix B: Mexico Cash Inflow Work Sheet

CASH INFLOW	4/2002	1/2003	2/2003	3/2003	4/2003	1/2004	2/2004	3/2004	4/2004	1/2005	2/2005	3/2005	4/2005
Sales													
Cash Account													
Accounts Receivable													
Short-Term Investments													
Short-Term Loan													
Bond Sales													
Stock Sale													
Patents													
Subcontracting													
Capital Sales													
Liquidation/Salvaging													
Miscellaneous Credits													
Cash Transfers In													
Total Cash In													

CASH OUTFLOW	4/2002	1/2003	2/2003	3/2003	4/2003	1/2004	2/2004	3/2004	4/2004	1/2005	2/2005	3/2005	4/2005
Factory Wages													
Subassemblies Purchases													
Advertising													
General Administration													

Distribution Centers																								
Wholesalers/Sales Offices																								
Sales Force/Trainees																								
Training and Development																								
Inventory Charges																								
Shipping																								
Patent Fees																								
Subcontracting Cost																								
Research and Development																								
Quality Control/Programs																								
Maintenance																								
Income Tax																								
Accounts Payable																								
Overdraft Payment																								
Interest																								
Dividend																								
Bond Call/Treasury Stock																								
Capital In Progress																								
Cash Transfers Out																								
Total Cash Out																								
Cash Surplus/Deficit																								

Appendix B: Germany Cash Inflow Work Sheet

CASH INFLOW	4/2002	1/2003	2/2003	3/2003	4/2003	1/2004	2/2004	3/2004	4/2004	1/2005	2/2005	3/2005	4/2005
Sales													
Cash Account													
Accounts Receivable													
Short-Term Investments													
Short-Term Loan													
Bond Sales													
Stock Sale													
Patents													
Subcontracting													
Capital Sales													
Liquidation/Salvaging													
Miscellaneous Credits													
Cash Transfers In													
Total Cash In													

CASH OUTFLOW	4/2002	1/2003	2/2003	3/2003	4/2003	1/2004	2/2004	3/2004	4/2004	1/2005	2/2005	3/2005	4/2005
Factory Wages													
Subassemblies Purchases													
Advertising													
General Administration													

Distribution Centers																		
Wholesalers/Sales Offices																		
Sales Force/Trainees																		
Training and Development																		
Inventory Charges																		
Shipping																		
Patent Fees																		
Subcontracting Cost																		
Research and Development																		
Quality Control/Programs																		
Maintenance																		
Income Tax																		
Accounts Payable																		
Overdraft Payment																		
Interest																		
Dividend																		
Bond Call/Treasury Stock																		
Capital In Progress																		
Cash Transfers Out																		
Total Cash Out																		
Cash Surplus/Deficit																		

Appendix B: Spain Cash Inflow Work Sheet

CASH INFLOW	4/2002	1/2003	2/2003	3/2003	4/2003	1/2004	2/2004	3/2004	4/2004	1/2005	2/2005	3/2005	4/2005
Sales													
Cash Account													
Accounts Receivable													
Short-Term Investments													
Short-Term Loan													
Bond Sales													
Stock Sale													
Patents													
Subcontracting													
Capital Sales													
Liquidation/Salvaging													
Miscellaneous Credits													
Cash Transfers In													
Total Cash In													

CASH OUTFLOW	4/2002	1/2003	2/2003	3/2003	4/2003	1/2004	2/2004	3/2004	4/2004	1/2005	2/2005	3/2005	4/2005
Factory Wages													
Subassemblies Purchases													
Advertising													
General Administration													

Distribution Centers	
Wholesalers/Sales Offices	
Sales Force/Trainees	
Training and Development	
Inventory Charges	
Shipping	
Patent Fees	
Subcontracting Cost	
Research and Development	
Quality Control/Programs	
Maintenance	
Income Tax	
Accounts Payable	
Overdraft Payment	
Interest	
Dividend	
Bond Call/Treasury Stock	
Capital In Progress	
Cash Transfers Out	
Total Cash Out	
Cash Surplus/Deficit	

Appendix B: Japan Cash Inflow Work Sheet

CASH INFLOW	4/2002	1/2003	2/2003	3/2003	4/2003	1/2004	2/2004	3/2004	4/2004	1/2005	2/2005	3/2005	4/2005
Sales													
Cash Account													
Accounts Receivable													
Short-Term Investments													
Short-Term Loan													
Bond Sales													
Stock Sale													
Patents													
Subcontracting													
Capital Sales													
Liquidation/Salvaging													
Miscellaneous Credits													
Cash Transfers In													
Total Cash In													

CASH OUTFLOW	4/2002	1/2003	2/2003	3/2003	4/2003	1/2004	2/2004	3/2004	4/2004	1/2005	2/2005	3/2005	4/2005
Factory Wages													
Subassemblies Purchases													
Advertising													
General Administration													

	Distribution Centers	Wholesalers/Sales Offices	Sales Force/Trainees	Training and Development	Inventory Charges	Shipping	Patent Fees	Subcontracting Cost	Research and Development	Quality Control/Programs	Maintenance	Income Tax	Accounts Payable	Overdraft Payment	Interest	Dividend	Bond Call/Treasury Stock	Capital In Progress	Cash Transfers Out	Total Cash Out	Cash Surplus/Deficit

Appendix B: Thailand Cash Inflow Work Sheet

CASH INFLOW	4/2002	1/2003	2/2003	3/2003	4/2003	1/2004	2/2004	3/2004	4/2004	1/2005	2/2005	3/2005	4/2005
Sales													
Cash Account													
Accounts Receivable													
Short-Term Investments													
Short-Term Loan													
Bond Sales													
Stock Sale													
Patents													
Subcontracting													
Capital Sales													
Liquidation/Salvaging													
Miscellaneous Credits													
Cash Transfers In													
Total Cash In													

CASH OUTFLOW	4/2002	1/2003	2/2003	3/2003	4/2003	1/2004	2/2004	3/2004	4/2004	1/2005	2/2005	3/2005	4/2005
Factory Wages													
Subassemblies Purchases													
Advertising													
General Administration													

Distribution Centers																					
Wholesalers/Sales Offices																					
Sales Force/Trainees																					
Training and Development																					
Inventory Charges																					
Shipping																					
Patent Fees																					
Subcontracting Cost																					
Research and Development																					
Quality Control/Programs																					
Maintenance																					
Income Tax																					
Accounts Payable																					
Overdraft Payment																					
Interest																					
Dividend																					
Bond Call/Treasury Stock																					
Capital In Progress																					
Cash Transfers Out																					
Total Cash Out																					
Cash Surplus/Deficit																					

Appendix C: *Pro Forma* Income Statements

United States

Revenues:	1/2003	2/2003	3/2003	4/2003	1/2004	2/2004	3/2004	4/2004
Gross Revenues								
Value-Added Tax								
Net Sales								
Other Income:								
Capital Gains/Losses								
Investment Income								
Licenses/Subcontracting								
Non-Operating Income								
Total Revenue								
Expenses:								
Cost of Goods Sold								
Advertising								
General Administration								
Sales Offices								
Distribution Centers								
Wholesale Operations								
Sales Force Salaries								
Trainees								
Training and Development								
Inventory Charges								
Shipping								
License Fees								
Research and Development								
Quality Control								
Depreciation								
Maintenance								
Interest Charges:								
Overdrafts								
Short-Term Loan								
Bonds								
Miscellaneous								
Total Expenses								
Income Before Taxes								
Income Tax								
Dividend Tax								
Net Income								

Appendix C: *Pro Forma* **Income Statements**

Mexico

Revenues:	1/2003	2/2003	3/2003	4/2003	1/2004	2/2004	3/2004	4/2004
Gross Revenues								
Value-Added Tax								
Net Sales								
Other Income:								
Capital Gains/Losses								
Investment Income								
Licenses/Subcontracting								
Non-Operating Income								
Total Revenue								
Expenses:								
Cost of Goods Sold								
Advertising								
General Administration								
Sales Offices								
Distribution Centers								
Wholesale Operations								
Sales Force Salaries								
Trainees								
Training and Development								
Inventory Charges								
Shipping								
License Fees								
Research and Development								
Quality Control								
Depreciation								
Maintenance								
Interest Charges:								
Overdrafts								
Short-Term Loan								
Bonds								
Miscellaneous								
Total Expenses								
Income Before Taxes								
Income Tax								
Dividend Tax								
Net Income								

Appendix C: *Pro Forma* Income Statements

Germany

Revenues:	1/2003	2/2003	3/2003	4/2003	1/2004	2/2004	3/2004	4/2004
Gross Revenues								
Value-Added Tax								
Net Sales								
Other Income:								
Capital Gains/Losses								
Investment Income								
Licenses/Subcontracting								
Non-Operating Income								
Total Revenue								
Expenses:								
Cost of Goods Sold								
Advertising								
General Administration								
Sales Offices								
Distribution Centers								
Wholesale Operations								
Sales Force Salaries								
Trainees								
Training and Development								
Inventory Charges								
Shipping								
License Fees								
Research and Development								
Quality Control								
Depreciation								
Maintenance								
Interest Charges:								
Overdrafts								
Short-Term Loan								
Bonds								
Miscellaneous								
Total Expenses								
Income Before Taxes								
Income Tax								
Dividend Tax								
Net Income								

Appendix C: *Pro Forma* Income Statements

Spain

Revenues:	1/2003	2/2003	3/2003	4/2003	1/2004	2/2004	3/2004	4/2004
Gross Revenues								
Value-Added Tax								
Net Sales								
Other Income:								
Capital Gains/Losses								
Investment Income								
Licenses/Subcontracting								
Non-Operating Income								
Total Revenue								
Expenses:								
Cost of Goods Sold								
Advertising								
General Administration								
Sales Offices								
Distribution Centers								
Wholesale Operations								
Sales Force Salaries								
Trainees								
Training and Development								
Inventory Charges								
Shipping								
License Fees								
Research and Development								
Quality Control								
Depreciation								
Maintenance								
Interest Charges:								
Overdrafts								
Short-Term Loan								
Bonds								
Miscellaneous								
Total Expenses								
Income Before Taxes								
Income Tax								
Dividend Tax								
Net Income								

Appendix C: *Pro Forma* Income Statements

Japan

Revenues:	1/2003	2/2003	3/2003	4/2003	1/2004	2/2004	3/2004	4/2004
Gross Revenues								
Value-Added Tax								
Net Sales								
Other Income:								
Capital Gains/Losses								
Investment Income								
Licenses/Subcontracting								
Non-Operating Income								
Total Revenue								
Expenses:								
Cost of Goods Sold								
Advertising								
General Administration								
Sales Offices								
Distribution Centers								
Wholesale Operations								
Sales Force Salaries								
Trainees								
Training and Development								
Inventory Charges								
Shipping								
License Fees								
Research and Development								
Quality Control								
Depreciation								
Maintenance								
Interest Charges:								
Overdrafts								
Short-Term Loan								
Bonds								
Miscellaneous								
Total Expenses								
Income Before Taxes								
Income Tax								
Dividend Tax								
Net Income								

Appendix C: *Pro Forma* Income Statements

Thailand

Revenues:	1/2003	2/2003	3/2003	4/2003	1/2004	2/2004	3/2004	4/2004
Gross Revenues								
Value-Added Tax								
Net Sales								
Other Income:								
Capital Gains/Losses								
Investment Income								
Licenses/Subcontracting								
Non-Operating Income								
Total Revenue								
Expenses:								
Cost of Goods Sold								
Advertising								
General Administration								
Sales Offices								
Distribution Centers								
Wholesale Operations								
Sales Force Salaries								
Trainees								
Training and Development								
Inventory Charges								
Shipping								
License Fees								
Research and Development								
Quality Control								
Depreciation								
Maintenance								
Interest Charges:								
Overdrafts								
Short-Term Loan								
Bonds								
Miscellaneous								
Total Expenses								
Income Before Taxes								
Income Tax								
Dividend Tax								
Net Income								

Appendix D: *Pro Forma* Balance Sheets

United States

Assets:	1/2003	2/2003	3/2003	4/2003	1/2004	2/2004	3/2004	4/2004
Cash								
Accounts Receivable								
Tax Credit								
Short-Term Investments								
Due From Country Unit(s)								
Inventories:								
Subassemblies								
Finished Goods								
Goods In Transit								
Total Current Assets								
Capital In Progress								
Plant and Equipment								
Less Depreciation								
Total Fixed Assets								
Total Assets								
Liabilities and Owner's Equity:								
Accounts Payable								
Overdraft								
Due to Home Country								
Short-Term Loan								
Total Current Liabilities								
Bonds								
Total Liabilities								
Stockholdler's Equity:								
Common Stock								
Paid-In Capital								
Retained Earnings/Deficit								
Exhange Gains/Losses								
Total Stockholder's Equity								
Total Liabilities and Owner's Equity								

Appendix D: *Pro Forma* Balance Sheets

Mexico

Assets:	1/2003	2/2003	3/2003	4/2003	1/2004	2/2004	3/2004	4/2004
Cash								
Accounts Receivable								
Tax Credit								
Short-Term Investments								
Due From Country Unit(s)								
Inventories:								
Subassemblies								
Finished Goods								
Goods In Transit								
Total Current Assets								
Capital In Progress								
Plant and Equipment								
Less Depreciation								
Total Fixed Assets								
Total Assets								
Liabilities and Owner's Equity:								
Accounts Payable								
Overdraft								
Due to Home Country								
Short-Term Loan								
Total Current Liabilities								
Bonds								
Total Liabilities								
Stockholdler's Equity:								
Common Stock								
Paid-In Capital								
Retained Earnings/Deficit								
Exhange Gains/Losses								
Total Stockholder's Equity								
Total Liabilities and Owner's Equity								

Appendix D: *Pro Forma* Balance Sheets

Germany

Assets:	1/2003	2/2003	3/2003	4/2003	1/2004	2/2004	3/2004	4/2004
Cash								
Accounts Receivable								
Tax Credit								
Short-Term Investments								
Due From Country Unit(s)								
Inventories:								
Subassemblies								
Finished Goods								
Goods In Transit								
Total Current Assets								
Capital In Progress								
Plant and Equipment								
Less Depreciation								
Total Fixed Assets								
Total Assets								
Liabilities and Owner's Equity:								
Accounts Payable								
Overdraft								
Due to Home Country								
Short-Term Loan								
Total Current Liabilities								
Bonds								
Total Liabilities								
Stockholdler's Equity:								
Common Stock								
Paid-In Capital								
Retained Earnings/Deficit								
Exhange Gains/Losses								
Total Stockholder's Equity								
Total Liabilities and Owner's Equity								

Appendix D: *Pro Forma* Balance Sheets

Spain

Assets:	1/2003	2/2003	3/2003	4/2003	1/2004	2/2004	3/2004	4/2004
Cash								
Accounts Receivable								
Tax Credit								
Short-Term Investments								
Due From Country Unit(s)								
Inventories:								
Subassemblies								
Finished Goods								
Goods In Transit								
Total Current Assets								
Capital In Progress								
Plant and Equipment								
Less Depreciation								
Total Fixed Assets								
Total Assets								
Liabilities and Owner's Equity:								
Accounts Payable								
Overdraft								
Due to Home Country								
Short-Term Loan								
Total Current Liabilities								
Bonds								
Total Liabilities								
Stockholdler's Equity:								
Common Stock								
Paid-In Capital								
Retained Earnings/Deficit								
Exhange Gains/Losses								
Total Stockholder's Equity								
Total Liabilities and Owner's Equity								

Appendix D: *Pro Forma* Balance Sheets

Japan

Assets:	1/2003	2/2003	3/2003	4/2003	1/2004	2/2004	3/2004	4/2004
Cash								
Accounts Receivable								
Tax Credit								
Short-Term Investments								
Due From Country Unit(s)								
Inventories:								
Subassemblies								
Finished Goods								
Goods In Transit								
Total Current Assets								
Capital In Progress								
Plant and Equipment								
Less Depreciation								
Total Fixed Assets								
Total Assets								
Liabilities and Owner's Equity:								
Accounts Payable								
Overdraft								
Due to Home Country								
Short-Term Loan								
Total Current Liabilities								
Bonds								
Total Liabilities								
Stockholdler's Equity:								
Common Stock								
Paid-In Capital								
Retained Earnings/Deficit								
Exhange Gains/Losses								
Total Stockholder's Equity								
Total Liabilities and Owner's Equity								

Appendix D: *Pro Forma* **Balance Sheets**

Thailand

Assets:	1/2003	2/2003	3/2003	4/2003	1/2004	2/2004	3/2004	4/2004
Cash								
Accounts Receivable								
Tax Credit								
Short-Term Investments								
Due From Country Unit(s)								
Inventories:								
Subassemblies								
Finished Goods								
Goods In Transit								
Total Current Assets								
Capital In Progress								
Plant and Equipment								
Less Depreciation								
Total Fixed Assets								
Total Assets								
Liabilities and Owner's Equity:								
Accounts Payable								
Overdraft								
Due to Home Country								
Short-Term Loan								
Total Current Liabilities								
Bonds								
Total Liabilities								
Stockholdler's Equity:								
Common Stock								
Paid-In Capital								
Retained Earnings/Deficit								
Exhange Gains/Losses								
Total Stockholder's Equity								
Total Liabilities and Owner's Equity								

Appendix E: Critical Incidents

CRITICAL INCIDENT 1   BILL FISHER'S NEW SALARY BONUS SYSTEM

After serving in your company's Chicago sales office as the area's top sales representative for five years, Bill Fisher was moved to your South Jersey district sales office in Trenton, New Jersey, four months ago to improve its below-average performance. After looking over his salespersons' records and getting to know each better by going on calls with them, he was concerned that some were not as productive as he felt they could be. He also sensed that many, especially the district's senior reps, had fallen into old patterns, weren't looking for new business, and needed to improve their selling techniques.

Bill felt the crux of the problem came from how the company's sales bonuses were calculated. As he explained, "The system we have now is the traditional one. I sit down with the rep at the beginning of the year and we set what we agree are reasonable sales goals. If reps beat the goal, they get the bonus. If they don't . . . no bonus. While this all sounds straightforward, it's much more complicated than that. We spend a lot of time arguing over what's a reasonable goal. Even worse, most reps meet the goal, but I think they could do even more."

To fix the situation, Bill has devised what he calls the Market Share Gain Plan. Under this system, each sale rep is ranked against all the other district reps regarding the market shares of the company's television sets they produce in their sales area. Bill reasoned, "We live and die on market share, and we have to increase our market penetration. What I'm doing is rewarding those who produce what we need. Those who increase their market shares the most get the biggest bonuses, and those who lose market share get closer supervision from me. That way they'll be able to do better next season. If they ultimately don't improve after all my help, I'm afraid I'd have to let them go."

Before implementing his system, Fisher paid a courtesy call to the Human Resources Management Department because of his plan's payroll ramifications. Despite his enthusiasm, the HRM Department cautioned him about certain potential problems.

Those who receive Bill's "help" after not getting their bonuses might consider this a form of punishment or a way of singling them out for ridicule among their peers. The ability of a single sales rep to produce market share gains was also thought to be problematical. To some degree, your company's market share in any sales area is a function of the quality and prices of the sets being offered by your competitors. A sales representative has no control over this. More important, some in the HRM Department felt Bill's system might discriminate against older sales reps, as they had established market shares, whereas new sales reps started out from low market shares, which might be more easily increased.

Responses

1. Let Bill Fisher implement his Market Share Gain Plan. He believes most reps will get some type of bonus and that those who don't "make bonus" might get one the following year after his help. It is believed this option would generate additional profits of $250,000 and would appear as a credit to your miscellaneous account for the quarter.
2. Let Bill Fisher implement his Market Share Gain Plan on a trial basis in two separate New Jersey sales areas, with one area under the control of one of your senior sales reps and the other under the control of a junior sales representative. This option would cost your firm $15,000 and would appear as an additional one-quarter sales force expense.
3. Step back and have Bill present his Market Share Gain Plan at a district meeting of all sales representatives to get their feedback. It is believed strong objections would be heard from your older sales reps, but they make up only 25 percent of the district's selling staff. The cost of this option would be $110,000, which is the value Bill puts on the lost margins he thinks his plan would produce if implemented immediately.
4. Don't implement the plan and concentrate on improving the selling techniques of all sales representatives. This option requires you to spend at least $10,000 per country on sales rep training for the next four consecutive quarters.

CRITICAL INCIDENT 2   *"YOU HAVE TO GET THEIR ATTENTION"*

John Englehart threw off his jacket, loosened his tie, and said to no one in particular, "Trying to sell our sets cold canvas is really frustrating. What we need is something that will get our foot in the door so we can make our pitch."

Englehart's complaint received a sympathetic response from the sales office's other sales reps. They all had spent many idle hours trying to see the retail buyers who might buy your TVs. As John asserted, "To make a sale you have to get their attention. If we can just do that, we can sell more goods, and make it easier to get our commissions, and we'll stop wasting time cooling our heels in waiting rooms. Let's all try to brainstorm this thing. I'm sure we can come up with some good ideas."

On that note a number of notions were bandied about. Helen Fernandez suggested putting together a mailing list of the market's major retailers who were not stocking your company's sets. Mike Hardaway tagged onto that idea, but suggested that some type of gift with the letter might really get the buyers' attention. "Why not offer everyone on the list $35 for an appointment? I've heard some other companies have done this with pretty good results." "I don't know about that idea, Mike," Helen responded. "That sort of sounds like a bribe to me or that we're really desperate." "Well, maybe we can tone it down a bit, or be more subtle, but I think we're on the right track. Any more good ideas?" John asked. "What do you think we should do?"

Responses

1. Send out a mailing offering a straight $30 cash gift to no more than 400 retail buyers whose stores do not stock your sets. The entire charge of $14,000 will be billed to your firm's sales force expense for the quarter.
2. Combine the above mailing list with a list of all retailers presently stocking your sets. Offer all recipients an appropriate "Seasons Greetings" gift valued at about $20. In a form letter, thank all those who are stocking your sets for their business, with wishes for a successful New Year. For those not stocking your TVs, indicate you will be contacting them soon to show them how to have an even more successful coming year by stocking your sets. The entire cost of $55,000 for this mailing will be billed to your firm's sales force expense for the quarter.
3. Send a letter offering all retailers not stocking your sets a $50 rebate on the first order they place with your company. On this order only they will also receive an additional $2 special allowance for each set purchased. You estimate about 100 retailers will respond with an appointment and that the average order will be for twelve sets. The entire cost of this option will be added to your firm's sales office expense in the current quarter.
4. Increase the space of your company's booth at the upcoming Home Electronics Trade Show in New York City's Javits Trade Center. Invite every retailer in all your markets to visit your "Hospitality Center" when they are at the trade show. The cost of this response will add $35,000 to your firm's advertising expense for the quarter.

CRITICAL INCIDENT 3   *THE NEW AUTOMATON TECHNICIAN*

One of your brightest, up-and-coming younger workers is having some on-the-job problems. Consuelo Hernandez came to your company as a secretary right after graduating with a community college degree in secretarial science. She had real hands-on knowledge of every piece of equipment and all software associated with the modern business office. Consuelo quickly fit in because of her cheerful personality and willingness to learn.

From the very start of her employment, she made it clear, but in a very nice manner, that she was ambitious and was willing to try anything that would promote her career and give her a well-rounded view of your firm's operations. Because of her skills and energy level, after three years Consuelo had grown beyond her job requirements but could not assume executive secretary or office manager status because very competent people with greater seniority already occupied these positions.

Rather than losing her to some other company, and because it was believed her knowledge of programmable software and practical computer savvy would transfer to the skill requirement side of an automaton technician's job, Consuelo was offered such a position. As you had expected, Consuelo gladly accepted the challenge, as it gave her exposure to the factory side of your operations, a totally new line of advancement, and a pay raise.

As Consuelo had done in your office, she quickly caught onto the job's requirements after going through a short technical training program conducted off-site by your automaton manufacturer. *That* was not the problem. What *was* the problem were complaints she has brought to you about the hazing she was being subjected to, much of it verbally and graphically sexually suggestive. When probed about the comments and cat-calls yelled out by line workers as she passed through the factory, Consuelo broke down crying and handed you a sheaf of crudely scrawled notes and cardboard signs that made all sorts of sexual propositions to her.

Before taking any action in this regard, you and your plant superintendent toured your Erie, Pennsylvania, factory to follow up on Consuelo's view of the situation. An inspection of the factory's walls and girder columns found them to be clean, freshly painted, and free of graffiti. The walls and stalls in the men's restroom, however, were covered with felt-tipped pornographic messages and pictures, a few of which listed Consuelo's home telephone number and a list of the "services" she would provide.

As your tour continued later in the day, the plant superintendent observed, "Boys will be boys," and said that the male line workers were just having a little fun to break up the monotony of their jobs. As far as he was concerned, they did not mean any harm and "Consuelo should learn how to take it." When asked what should be done about the situation, your superintendent replied, "Look, I can talk to the guys and tell them to knock it off. I don't know if it will do any good, though. She sort of causes the problem herself. You know, it's those tight T-shirts she wears. It's okay for guys to wear them in here because of all the heat, but for her to wear one—that's just asking for trouble. What I want to know from you is why did you have to put such a good-looking gal in here in the first place!"

Based on this information, what do you believe is your best course of action? You are aware of the recent U.S. Supreme Court ruling that employers must ensure their general work environments are free of sexual harassment and that class action suits by the government are appropriate when such conditions are not being met in the victims' eyes. You are also aware that your female assembly line workers, who make up about 25 percent of these workers, are following Consuelo's case with great interest.

Responses

1. Have your plant superintendent hold a meeting of all line workers to remind them that sexual comments, and the display of pornography, violate your company's standing policies intended to ensure that a sexual harassment–free environment exists in all work spaces. This option, taken for one-half hour on company time, results in a non-significant cost to your firm.

2. Hold a mandatory three-part weekly series of workshops and plant conferences on sexual harassment. These one-hour meetings would be held on company time at the beginning of Wednesday's plant operations and would cost your home country plant US$140,000 for training and estimated lost-productivity costs for the current quarter. The charge would be processed through your miscellaneous account.

3. Advise Consuelo that you understand the pressure under which she has been placed. Caution her, however, that there are always "two sides to every story" and that she may be partially the cause of her trouble. Suggest to her that she be more circumspect about her attire in the factory and offer to return her to her former secretarial position. This action causes your firm no out-of-pocket expense.

4. Fire your plant superintendent as a demonstration "that you mean business" about sexual harassment and that he has failed to enforce your company's harassment-free policy. This response will cost your firm US$120,000 through your current quarter's miscellaneous account for the "early retirement" of this superintendent.

CRITICAL INCIDENT 4 *HOW TO IMPLEMENT A STRUCTURAL CHANGE*

"Look, we're going to have to change who pays these warranty costs we're getting sooner or later, so I say let's do it now and get it over with as fast as possible." With these words Tim Martinko, your company's marketing director, summarized how he would go about changing who is really responsible for minimizing warranty work and its costs.

Almost the opposite tack was being suggested by your operations manager, Joe Graham, and your quality control supervisor, David Hubanks. "It took a long time for this problem to develop, so it'll take a long time for it to be resolved," David observed. "I think we should go about this slowly, so everybody feels comfortable about what has to be done."

After much wrangling over who was accountable for the warranty charges currently being absorbed by your distribution centers, the argument has finally come down to these polar positions. In its desire to be fast in its response to problems with defective sets, your company set up repair facilities as close to your customers as possible. It was felt this would be at the distribution center level, where control over repairs would be stronger, as opposed to the wholesaler level. Once these repair facilities had been established in your distribution centers, it was logical to have the centers pay for the warranty repairs, as they were doing the work. Also, by having them bear these expenses, they would be encouraged to minimize these costs as much as possible.

Over the years, however, your distribution centers have started to feel they are bearing the brunt of having to fix TVs they think your plants should have made right in the first place. They also have reasoned that by having the distribution centers fix whatever is wrong with the sets, the plants have no incentive to minimize assembly errors.

So far no decision has been made about how to solve this problem. As the person in charge of implementing whatever change is ultimately decided upon, however, which of the following do you think would be the best course of action for you to take?

Responses

1. Rather than changing who pays for the warranty repairs, take action to minimize any off-quality TVs coming out of your factories. Demonstrate to your distribution centers your good faith in this regard by guaranteeing that every plant's quality control program will be at the maximum level from this quarter forward. This response will cost your firm the price of the standard C sample size quality control program in addition to the quality control supervisor's regular US$10,000 quarterly salary.
2. Rather than changing who pays for the warranty repairs, have all defective television sets shipped ExAir, for the fastest customer service possible, to their factories of origin. All shipping charges, inventory and handling charges, and warranty repair costs will be borne by the factory involved. This procedure would continue for the remainder of the simulation.
3. Have each distribution center continue to repair all sets under warranty, but have the repair charges paid by each factory of origin. This option merely switches who pays for the repairs. Accordingly, all warranty repair costs would be charged to your firm's general administration expense for the remainder of the game.
4. Delay determining who pays for the warranty work costs for one quarter. Create a warranty work task force made up of relevant personnel from your distribution centers, Quality Control Department, and line supervisors. Their task would be to create in one quarter a mutually agreeable payment method, the only constraint being that the solution must result in optimal service to customers who have brought their sets in for repairs. It is assumed this option will not produce new out-of-pocket costs to your firm.

CRITICAL INCIDENT 5   *FERDIE MILANO FIGHTS BACK*

At the beginning of the 1999 selling year, Bill Fisher implemented his new Market Share Gain Plan. This system rated sales reps on the market shares they produced in each of their sales areas. Many of the younger reps liked the system and reaped sizable bonuses. Ferdinand ("Ferdie") Milano, however, was struggling. Once the district's top salesperson, he was now ranked at the bottom, and this was vexing to both him and Bill Fisher. Ferdie was mad because he was no longer getting bonuses, and Bill was frustrated because he had spent many fruitless hours trying to turn Ferdie around.

Bill had made a number of dual calls with Ferdie and had worked with him on his sales presentations. He also mailed him technical literature describing advances in electronics technology and how those advances made the company's sets more competitive. Ferdie didn't respond well to these suggestions and said to others that he was "in Bill's doghouse" and might lose his job.

The breaking point came when Bill happened to be in Ferdie's Lawrenceville, New Jersey, neighborhood at about 9:30 A.M. on other business. As he drove by, he saw the company's gray car in the driveway even though all sales reps were supposed to be "on territory" by that time. Because he suspected something was wrong, and Ferdie had been submitting territory activity reports showing he was making calls every morning by 8 A.M., Bill started to make regular checks. More often than not, the company car was in the driveway.

This was enough for Bill. Over coffee and doughnuts at their favorite diner on a Thursday morning, he handed Ferdie a dismissal notice effective immediately. Bill then followed Ferdie home, where he told him to hand over the company car keys as well as the company's sales literature. Ferdie was brokenhearted and humiliated and stated in no uncertain terms that he "was not going to take this lying down" and that his "life had been ruined."

The Newark, New Jersey, law firm of McDuff & Rice has just served your company with notice that its client Ferdinand Milano is threatening a lawsuit. The terms of the settlement would be reinstatement of his position, three months' back wages, $750,000 for pain and suffering, the payment of all associated legal fees filed by McDuff & Rice, a written apology from Bill Fisher, and the revocation of your company's Market Share Gain Plan. If these terms were not met, McDuff & Rice would file on Milano's behalf a 13-count age discrimination complaint. Under N.J.S.A. 10:51-2(d), the New Jersey Law against Discrimination, it would be claimed that your company created a motivation system that was prejudiced against its senior sales representatives and that you fired Ferdie in retaliation for not accepting your firm's Voluntary Enhanced Retirement Program offered earlier in the year.

Responses

1. Settle out of court by accepting all of Ferdie Milano's terms. This option would cost your firm $771,450, which would appear as a miscellaneous expense for the current quarter.
2. Negotiate with the law firm, assuming their terms are just "talking points." You can assume the negotiations would last six months, during which back wages would mount but Ferdie might ultimately settle for $350,000 and no job reinstatement. This amount would show as an expense of $350,000 for the present quarter.
3. Allow the lawsuit to go to a jury trial in the State of New Jersey. Your company lawyers believe they would win the case, based on Ferdie's lack of response to Bill's efforts to rehabilitate him and the fact that many sales reps have done well under the new bonus system. Should you lose the case, which your lawyers believe is unlikely, they think a jury's award for this case might range from $1.5 to $2.5 million. An amount comparable to awards given for such cases would appear as an expense item in the current quarter's miscellaneous account.
4. Launch a countersuit for $500,000 plus court costs against Ferdie Milano and the law firm of McDuff & Rice. In your lawsuit, you are claiming (1) the filing of inappropriate and exorbitant lawyers' fees by McDuff & Rice as part of the possible out-of-court settlement and (2) defamation of Bill Fisher's character by Ferdie in public statements he has made about his former boss and your company. If successful, this response would result in a net credit of $500,000 to your firm's miscellaneous account in the current quarter.

CRITICAL INCIDENT 6   *"HELL NO TO THIS* BAKSHEESH *STUFF!"*

You have recently sent Robert Frazier, one of your country liaison executives, around the world with your operations manager, Joseph Graham, to scout possible new plant locations. They are now summarizing for you their estimation of the prospects for building new plants overseas.

"As far as I can see, we have a large number of choices, especially in Asia, which is also closest to our Hong Kong supplier." Bob Frazier continued, "Our labor costs would be very low and the infrastructures available to us would be adequate for an assembly operation like ours."

"I have to agree with you on that," Joe Graham responded. "But I have a real problem with some other things, especially with the ethics some of those foreign businessmen showed me. And I thought it was even worse in the case of some of the government people we met."

"Well, you'll just have to get used to that . . . they've operated this way for years and that's how it's done over there." Bob leaned across the table to emphasize his point. "Even more, it's good to get on their good side, and a little bit of *baksheesh* can save you a whole lot of time and money in the long run."

This comment seemed to trigger an anger that had been boiling inside Joe all during the trip. "I don't care if you call it *blat, baksheesh,* or *grease!* It's all illegal, and I don't think we should have any part of it. It just galls me that we have to line the pocket of some puny little bureaucrat just to process some papers that he's supposed to do in the first place! I know there has to be a law somewhere against this."

On that note a rambling discussion ensued. It was pointed out that the U.S. Foreign Corrupt Practices Act of 1977 allows for personal payments to foreign government and company officials as gratuities for performing "nondiscretionary" services or engaging in activities that are appropriately within the scope of their job descriptions. In this case, a small payment is not illegal. It was pointed out, however, that problems arise over what are considered "small" versus "large" payments, and what are "nondiscretionary" versus "discretionary" actions or are actions outside the scope of the official's strict job duties.

Given that your company may eventually build a plant in a country where you will face this problem, what position do you think your company should take?

Responses

1. Avoid building any new plants in Asia, where the practice of *baksheesh* is widespread.
2. Avoid breaking any American laws by conducting all negotiations on plant sites in a "neutral" nation such as Liechtenstein, Vanuatu, the Netherlands Antilles, or the Cayman Islands, where such activities are not illegal or are not monitored closely. This option would add the equivalent of US$250,000 to the cost of constructing your next plant in either Japan or Thailand and would be amortized along with the original investment expense.
3. Be practical and follow the "rules of the road" and deal with the problem on a plant-by-plant and country-by-country basis. This response would cause your miscellaneous account to be debited the equivalent of US$75,000 for each plant subsequently built in Thailand or Japan.
4. Hire local middlemen to represent your company in all negotiations with government officials and relevant businesspersons. This option would add US$80,000 to the cost of building any APEC factory.

CRITICAL INCIDENT 7   _JUMPING THE GUN, OR FAST TO MARKET?_

After seeing all your company's R&D monies for the past three quarters being pumped into developing a new comb filter circuit for your TV sets, your marketing director, Helen Monroe, wants the feature installed in all new units starting next quarter. While the technology itself is proven, has worked exceptionally well in prototype sets, and would be a real, marketable breakthrough for your line of TVs, a few assembly-related problems exist. The circuit itself, while on a smaller board, must be protected from heat and therefore requires the tricky insertion of a heat shield next to the unit on the TV's chassis. Therein lies the heated argument that is going on between Helen and Joe Graham, your operations management director.

Helen was summarizing her position for the group that had witnessed the debate. "I read in the _Wall Street Journal_ that Japan's carmakers take only 26 to 30 months to take their cars from concept to production with Mazda doing it in only 21 months. In the United States we take 29 to 46 months. Gillette introduces its products on a 2-year cycle instead of every 3 years as they did before—and because Bell Helicopter reduced its product-to-market time from 24 to 12 months it got a new $113.0 million contract for army training helicopters. You know the early bird gets the worm. We can't sit on this feature even if we have a few little problems putting the set together. Let me propose this—we can 'up' our quality control budget to catch any sets that don't work, and we can rebate to our distribution centers the unit repair costs of any sets above the norm that come back for warranty work. This way we'll beat the competition to market with something big, plus we've covered any assembly problems that might crop up."

Joe Graham responded, "I don't care what you read in the _Journal_ or about getting worms. All that speed to market hasn't kept Mazda from losing money year after year and losing market share to boot. Rushing products to market is really dangerous to your firm's quality image. Remember IBM had to recall the Warp version of its OS/2 after it came out? And what about all the bugs in first release of Windows® 95? I think we should wait another quarter to design some type of 'snap' assembly that combines the new comb filter circuit with the shield that is needed. Let's make haste slowly on this."

Given the need to get a payback on your R&D expenses, as well as the potential increases in sales that might accompany the introduction of your set's superior comb filter, which of the following alternatives do you want to implement?

Responses

1. Bring the product to market immediately. This option presents no out-of-pocket expenses to your firm.
2. Delay the introduction of the new feature for at least one quarter, during which any actual assembly problems associated with the installation of the new comb filter are worked out completely. This option costs your firm $85,000 for production-related R&D, which is charged to your company's general administration expense for one quarter.
3. Bring the product to market immediately, and also contract for a C sample size quality control program, which would allow only 1.5 percent of all defective products to reach the market. The US$36,000 charge for a study of this size would be processed in the normal manner.
4. Bring the product to market immediately and budget a C sample size quality control program, and also rebate to your distribution centers warranty repair costs for half of all sets returned for the next two quarters.

CRITICAL INCIDENT 8 *MAKING OUR QUALITY CIRCLE PROGRAM WORK*

Your quality control supervisor, David Hubanks, has just summarized for you the results of one quarter's worth of quality circle meetings he's held. "I think the ideas that have come out of these meetings are pretty good and I think we can implement some of them. Although I think we can get even more participation in the future, what's most important now is getting our line workers thinking 'quality' and involved in the quality process. Unfortunately, even though we've paid our line people to attend our quality circle meetings after work Wednesday, our attendance has been uneven, and I don't think we have much momentum going for us."

When you asked him if he had any ideas about getting momentum and better meeting attendance, Hubanks responded, "A simple solution would be to hold our meetings during regular factory working hours at full pay. They're already here and we wouldn't be infringing on their leisure time, kid pick-up obligations, and supper time. I think this solution would deal with the problem of getting good attendance. On the other hand, I don't think it gets to the core issue of getting our workers to want to do things better or to realize that we *have* to do better to be competitive in this business."

"Well, then," you responded, "what are your thoughts about dealing with that?"

David Hubanks then provided you with four ways to motivate your assembly line workers to get involved in a company-wide Total Quality Management program. Which one of the following would you select?

Responses

1. Conduct all future quality circle meetings on company time, thereby demonstrating that you are serious about quality. Have the first four meetings chaired by a motivational-type speaker from the Crosby College of Quality. This response would cost you US$20,000 for the speaker and an estimated US$180,000 in lost productivity. All expenses would be charged to your firm's miscellaneous account.
2. Create a number of benchmarking groups who would visit other factories in the area using similar manufacturing and assembly techniques. These groups would report back to your quality circle meetings what they have discovered. This response would cost you US$65,000 for two quarters and would be part of your firm's miscellaneous costs.
3. Have an independent consultant do a survey feedback study to determine what your factory workers feel about job satisfaction, their attitudes, performance, organizational climate, and the quality of work relationships. The consultant would use the information to stimulate discussions during quality circle meetings on company time about organizational problems while ultimately generating a plan for organizational change. This alternative would cost your company US$35,000 for one quarter for the consultant, over and above estimated lost productivity costs of US$180,000 to your miscellaneous account for the rest of the simulation.
4. Demonstrate the need for change to your workers by bringing to your factory a panel of customers who have had repeated warranty work problems with sets. Use this customer feedback to promote discussions during subsequent quality circle meetings on company time on the need for change and the need for customer satisfaction. This response would cost your company US$4,000 for one quarter, in addition to US$180,000 in lost productivity per quarter for the remaining quarters of the game. These expenses would be charged to your miscellaneous account.

CRITICAL INCIDENT 9 *GETTING A BETTER GRASP OF THE MARKET*

Because your company's previous management group felt that international operations might be in its future, a well-regarded consulting firm had been retained to make recommendations on how to go about "internationalizing" your company. The prime focus of their effort was to give your company, which has always had a strong domestic product structure, the ability to understand foreign markets.

The consulting firm's basic recommendation was to create an International Division, which would consolidate in one unit the country liaison executives now part of your company's general administration expense. By housing these executives together, it was reasoned, they could more easily share general information while retaining the unique knowledge they possess about their particular country's business practices and culture. They would also be given new power to influence product development priorities within your firm's R&D operation. The new International Division would be headed by a vice-president who would report directly to your company's CEO and would have veto power over international capital appropriations and the rationing of television sets between domestic customers and any off-shore operations.

Given that your company might create an International Division, four ways have been suggested to increase its internal effectiveness after it has been created. Each one has its pros and cons.

Responses

1. Have the division grow in influence by doubling the number of liaison specialists per country. This decision will add to your general administration expense the equivalent of US$25,000 per quarter for each offshore country/market for the rest of the simulation.
2. Increase the division's influence by stationing your country specialists in the R&D Department, with a dual reporting relationship to the heads of the R&D Department and the International Division. This decision does not result in an out-of-pocket cost to your company.
3. Increase the division's influence by stationing your country specialists in the Marketing Department, with a dual reporting relationship to the heads of the Marketing Department and the International Division. This decision does not result in an out-of-pocket cost to your company.
4. Create cross-functional marketing and product development teams with it being mandatory that your country liaison specialists serve on those teams. Because of the time involved with these activities, one additional country liaison executive would have to be hired at the equivalent of US$25,000 per quarter. This expense would be added to your general administration expense.

CRITICAL INCIDENT 10   *"ARE OUR TVS REALLY GLOBAL?"*

The discussion about how to advertise your television sets overseas between your marketing director, Helen Monroe, and one of your country liaison executives, Corinna del Greco, was getting heated. Helen, trying to drive home her essential arguments, explained, "We're competing in a global industry. That basically means the same TV set can be sold around the world regardless of the country's nature. If you agree with me on that point, it means we should have a standard logotype and a universal advertising campaign for all our sets. Nowadays all TV sets are like commodities. They're basically the same on the outside and fundamentally the same inside. If there *is* a difference between the various brands, most consumers wouldn't know the difference or don't care to know. Even more important for us, we grind our TVs out like cookies, which drives down their costs because of the economies of scale we get by doing this. We should apply the same principle to our advertising campaign. By using the same ad campaign over and over again from country to country, we get our own economies of scale."

Corinna replied a bit more coolly but just as emphatically, "Are our TVs really as global as you seem to think they are? The TVs might be the same, but the world's markets aren't that simple. These might all be the same sets, but they mean different things to those living in different countries. Also, some features that are important in one country are not that important in other countries. For example, the remote controls that are so important to German and American consumers are not that important to those in Japan and Thailand. In fact, for those in Japan and Thailand a remote control is a liability, because it's expensive to replace their batteries all the time. I urge you to reconsider your position and let me help you design ad campaigns and themes that are uniquely identified with the needs of each of the foreign markets we hope to enter."

On that note, a number of graduated alternatives were jointly developed by Helen and Corinna over the next few weeks. Choose one of the following from the set they have presented to you.

Responses

1. Follow Helen's basic idea and use the same advertising theme in all markets. This suggestion entails a one-time advertising design cost of US$25,000, which is processed through your firm's miscellaneous account this quarter.
2. Create an advertising program that emphasizes the same logotype in all advertisements, with slight variations in pictorial layouts and body copy from country to country. This alternative entails a one-time advertising design cost of US$25,000, processed through your firm's miscellaneous account this quarter plus an additional US$4,000 charge for the number of foreign countries your game administrator has allowed your firm to consider for entry.
3. Develop an advertising program that employs a basic image and logotype but is differentiated by the major markets of NAFTA, EC, and APEC. This response costs your company US$25,000 for creating the campaign's basic image and logotype and US$7,000 for each of the major markets your game administrator has allowed your firm to consider for entry.
4. Follow Corinna's basic idea and create a different advertising theme for each market based on consumer research conducted in each country. This suggestion costs your company, for each country where your products are sold, the equivalent of US$7,000 for a consumer research study and an amount equal to US$25,000 for each unique advertisement required. A total charge of US$32,000 will be processed for each country currently being commercialized in the current quarter with the same amount being charged whenever a new country is entered.

Appendix F: Patent Licensing Agreement

TO: GBG Game Administrator

FROM: Firm_____

SUBJECT: Patent Licensing Agreement

DATE: _____

Our company would like to inform you that an agreement has been reached between our firm and _____ to transfer our new patent to them beginning in Quarter ___, 200___, for the sum of $_____. The following are each company's authorized signatories to this contract, with a summary of the terms we have agreed upon.

Implementation Date:

Quarter   _____

Year 200 _____

Cash Value: _____

Game Administrator Approval:

_____

Appendix G: Plant Capacity and Automaton Sale Agreement

TO: GBG Game Administrator

FROM: Firm_____

SUBJECT: Plant Capacity, Automaton Sale and Transfer Agreement

DATE: _____

Our company would like to inform you that an agreement has been reached between our firm and _____ to transfer a quantity of our fixed capital to them in Quarter ___, 200___, for the sum of $_____. The following are each company's authorized signatories to this contract, with a summary of the terms we have agreed upon.

TARGET COUNTRY	BASE CAPACITY	AUTO1S	AUTO2S

Implementation Date:

Quarter   _____

Year 200 _____

Total Cash Value: _____

Game Administrator Approval:

_____

Appendix H: Subcontracting Agreement

TO: GBG Game Administrator

FROM: Firm_____

SUBJECT: Subcontracting Agreement

DATE: _____

Our company would like to inform you that an agreement has been reached between our firm and _____ to transfer to them a quantity of our television sets with a Quality Grade Level at or above in Quarter ___, 200___, for the sum of $_____. The following are each company's authorized signatories to this contract, with a summary of the terms we have agreed upon.

TARGET COUNTRY	25″ SETS	27″ SETS

Minimum Quality Grade Level: _____

Implementation Date:

Quarter _____

Year 200 _____

Total Cash Value: _____

Game Administrator Approval:

_____

Appendix I: Game Debriefing Form

Industry: _____

Firm: _____

Please complete the following form to help you gain additional insight into the strategic management issues with which you were involved when you played *The Global Management Game*. Your instructor or game administrator may use this form to conduct a class discussion of the business game.

A. As a group, write a short statement as to the goals and grand strategy your company pursued in the simulation. Do this without looking at any of the materials you created for your management team when you began the game.

B. Now look back at your comany's original goals and initial strategy. Did they change over the course of the game? Why or why not?

C. Characterize the organization structure your company actually used on a day-by-day decision-making basis. What were the pros and cons of the organization structure you used?

Pros:

Cons:

D. From your experience with *The Global Business Game,* what do you believe are the key success factors for a firm in your simulated industry? What hints for success would you pass on to anyone who plays this game in the future— or what specific behaviors do you think they should avoid?

Key Success Factors:

E. Assuming another group of students will take over your company sooin, review your firm's original mission state- ment and revise it if necessary, based on your experience with teh game and the nature of the competitive forces at work in your particular industry.

End-Game Mission Statement

Index